Life By Other Means

CONTRIBUTORS

John Bayley

Patricia Beer

A. S. Byatt

Shirley Chew

Donald Davie

Douglas Dunn

David Ellis

Leonard Forster

P. N. Furbank

Russell Greenwood

Koh Tai Ann

Jeremy Lewis

Naomi Lewis

Derwent May

Blake Morrison

Peter Porter

David Rawlinson

Paul Theroux

Anthony Thwaite

William Walsh

Gavin Young

LIFE BY OTHER MEANS

Essays on D. J. Enright

Edited by
JACQUELINE SIMMS

Oxford New York
OXFORD UNIVERSITY PRESS
1990

Oxford University Press, Walton Street, Oxford OX2 6DP

Oxford New York Toronto
Delhi Bombay Calcutta Madras Karachi
Petaling Jaya Singapore Hong Kong Tokyo
Nairobi Dar es Salaam Cape Town
Melbourne Auckland

and associated companies in
Berlin Ibadan

Oxford is a trade mark of Oxford University Press

British Library Cataloguing in Publication Data
by other means: essays on D. J. Enright.
1. Poetry in English. Enright. D. J.—Critical studies
Simms, Jacqueline, 1940–
821'.914
ISBN 0–19–212989–9

Library of Congress Cataloging in Publication Data
Data available
ISBN 0–19–212989–9

Phototypeset by Dobbie Typesetting Ltd.
Printed in Great Britain by
Bookcraft (Bath) Ltd.
Midsomer Norton, Avon

Art, they say, continues life by other means—
How other are they?

('Poetical Justice')

CONTENTS

Introduction   ix

I

On *Academic Year*   3
ANTHONY THWAITE

Enright's Japan   9
RUSSELL GREENWOOD

The Mendicant Professor: A Self-confessed Liberal
   in Singapore   20
KOH TAI ANN

Dennis Enright: A Portrait   29
PAUL THEROUX

Scenes from Publishing Life   36
JEREMY LEWIS

It Is Too Easy for the Literary Man to Forget . . . :
   D. J. Enright as Book Reviewer   49
DERWENT MAY

Adding to Truth: The Anthologist at Work   56
DAVID RAWLINSON

Fandango with the Professor   62
GAVIN YOUNG

II

In and Out of the Movement   69
BLAKE MORRISON

'The Thunder of Humanity': D. J. Enright's Liberal
   Imagination   74
DOUGLAS DUNN

The Accents of Enright   88
  WILLIAM WALSH

A Humanist Poet?   97
  P. N. FURBANK

The Terrible Shears: More Notes on Nostalgia   105
  DAVID ELLIS

'The Facts of Life': Poem written on reading
  The Terrible Shears   117
  PATRICIA BEER

Shadow Play: D. J. Enright's Books for Children   118
  NAOMI LEWIS

I Rather Like the Sound of Foreign Languages like
  Ezra Pound   124
  PETER PORTER

Those Foreigners   137
  JOHN BAYLEY

A Faust Book   144
  LEONARD FORSTER

Hearing about Damnation   150
  DONALD DAVIE

A Sense of Religion: Enright's God   158
  A. S. BYATT

Untold Stories   175
  SHIRLEY CHEW

Select Bibliography   189
Notes on Contributors   191

INTRODUCTION

'A man's work belongs to others . . . He ought to be able to call his life his own.' With this salutary warning in our ears, we have collected a series of essays that, read in order, attempt to tell the story of some of the very various aspects of D. J. Enright's life, at home and abroad, and mostly—though not entirely—at work rather than at play. The first part of the book is a mixed group not so much of biographical accounts, as of 'scenes from a working life'; some of them are memoirs that embrace the writers' own careers as they crossed with Enright's. The second part consists of critical essays, mostly on the poetry which, despite novels, children's books, and criticism, is surely paramount.

Anthony Thwaite begins with the essay he wrote to accompany *Academic Year*,* Enright's first, and best, of four novels, set in Alexandria, where he taught from 1947 to 1950. Thwaite was not there at the time, of course, but his account can hardly be bettered as he sets the scene for the travels and teaching to come, as well as describing the novel itself, which he 'had remembered as much more of a comic turn . . . than in fact is the case. . . . Among the jokes and flippant observations, the book has a strong vein of melancholy, disgust, and even tragedy.' It was in Alexandria that Enright published his first small collection of poems, an illustrated pamphlet, *Season Ticket*.

In several essays there are backward glimpses of Downing College, and of the magazine *Scrutiny*, where his early critical writings appeared. His childhood is left to David Ellis in his essay on *The Terrible Shears: Scenes from a Twenties Childhood*, an autobiographical sequence Enright wrote much later, about his upbringing as a working-class child in Leamington, where he was born in 1920. From grammar school, where he found himself suddenly 'good at passing exams' (his own modest explanation), he won an exhibition to Cambridge, where he stayed until the War put paid to his studies. His tutor at Downing was F. R. Leavis. Enright, in almost Japanese manner, remains loyal to his professor,

---

* In the paperback edition only, reissued by Oxford University Press as a Twentieth-Century Classic (1985).

See the Select Bibliography for details of D. J. Enright's publications (p. 189).

while several critics seem automatically to overestimate the
influence of Leavis and the surrounding 'Scrutineers' on him.
Leavis encouraged him, and gave him his head to write about
German literature in *Scrutiny*. From early on, Enright was his own
man.

The essayists in this collection don't follow him everywhere—
not to Birmingham, where he taught in the Extra-mural
Department of the University (1950–3), nor to Berlin (1956–7), nor
indeed to London in gaps between posts abroad, which must have
been awkward times, though they could be used for visits to
publishers, and for renewing metropolitan literary contacts, which
risk becoming less 'real' when a writer is abroad for long.

His first Far Eastern post was in Japan and it seems to have
been a happy and very purposeful time: the East suited him. He
taught at Kōnan University for three years (1953–6). Vikram
Seth has said elsewhere that he feels two years' stay is the
minimum if one is to write about a foreign country.* Enright in
fact wrote his book on Japan half-way through his visit, though
he says in the foreword to *The World of Dew* (1955) that his
'ambition was to belong to that small and select band of people
who have lived in Japan without writing a book about it'. The
pressure came from the Japanese first, 'and there sprang up a
sort of "cold war" between the non-existent book and myself,
until I had to write the book to save myself from the ghost of it'.
While in Japan, he also translated an anthology of Western-style
poems from the Japanese. The friend who describes Enright's
Japan has (I suspect) rather underplayed his own somewhat
Mephistophelean role in Enright's life there.

Berlin came next, where he was a visiting lecturer at the Free
University (1956–7), and though there is no memoir of that stay,
John Bayley in his essay on Enright's style, 'Those Foreigners',
catches, as he says Enright does in his poems, the feeling of
Germany not so long after the war.

After applying for the post of Johore Professor of English in
Singapore—a job he was offered too late to accept first time
round—he went as British Council Professor to Chulalongkorn
University in Bangkok (1957–9), where: 'It was good to be back

---

* Vikram Seth, in 'A Writer's Perspective of Place', a paper read at Carmel,
California, in 1989.

in the East, even though for a while we caught ourselves
addressing taxi-drivers in bad German to start off with and then
in bad Japanese.' The Bangkok episode ended disastrously, as
Gavin Young relates, when returning one night with his wife after
a party, Enright was beaten up and arrested by drunken Thai
police in front of a brothel opposite his house. Enright tells the
story too, with a mixture of chagrin and hilarity, but also irritation,
in *Memoirs of a Mendicant Professor*, since, already unpopular for
smoking opium, or rather, for refusing to promise never to do
so, Enright now found himself sacked from the job in Bangkok
after only a year (but, luckily, only after he had signed a contract
for a second year).

And so to Singapore in 1960, where the Johore Professorship
of English had unexpectedly come up again after only two years.
Koh Tai Ann, a former pupil of Enright's (now teaching herself
at the National University of Singapore) gives a Singaporean
account of what became known as the 'Enright Affair', a squall
in a teacup that overflowed into a political tempest after Enright's
inaugural lecture. Seen from the local post-colonial point of view,
trouble was inevitable. Dr Koh's essay is followed by a portrait of
the Professor by Paul Theroux, who taught in Enright's department
during his last year in Singapore (1969). To Theroux's novelist
eyes, Enright was restless, increasingly uncomfortable with the
political pressures on the university, and with departmental
changes of direction that were being imposed from above. But
did he want to leave? In an interview in London years later, he
seemed still ambivalent: 'Time moves on. Singapore is a closed
chapter. . . . But I am not sure who closed it.'*

Enright was 50 when he resigned from Singapore and returned
to Britain, his teaching career abroad ended, by his own choice,
for (as Theroux points out) there seems to have been no shortage
of offers made to him. For two years he worked as co-editor of
Encounter, and for a couple of terms gave tutorials at Leeds
University; then in 1972 he began to work at Chatto & Windus
(his own publisher), where he became a full-time director in 1974.
Jeremy Lewis gives a wry inside-account of the Dickensian offices
and rather harrowing atmosphere at Chatto in those days, and
of Enright himself, by now seated at the desk of C. Day Lewis.

* *Straits Times*, Singapore, 21 July 1984. Interview by Teresa Ooi in London.

He must have worked hard to produce his seven or eight books of poems; a trilogy of children's novels (and poems)—of which Naomi Lewis gives a charming account here; reviews and essays collected into books of criticism; *The Alluring Problem: An Essay on Irony* (which deserves an essay to itself); and several anthologies, that have come from his old-fashioned typewriter.

The essays on the poetry begin with Blake Morrison's account of Enright's involvement 'in and out' of the Movement. Douglas Dunn describes his tough liberal stance, and appreciates Enright's hedonistic and mischief-making nature. The siren voice of Peter Porter attempts to lure us on to the rocks where 'the sound' of music and 'of foreign languages' may (he says) mean as much as 'sense and meaning' to a poet. It is a compelling essay, but it seems unlikely that Enright will follow . . . A. S. Byatt analyses the 'sense of religion'—sad and unorthodox—that for better or for worse has persisted in his work; Donald Davie re-emphasizes this in a review of the *Collected Poems* of 1981, reproduced here. With P. N. Furbank on the nature of humanism in poetry, and Leonard Forster on *A Faust Book*, most aspects of Enright's poetry are included.

After the appearance of the *Collected Poems*, Enright was awarded the Queen's Medal for Poetry. His poems were by now published by Oxford University Press, but the event was fittingly celebrated by Norah Smallwood—publisher of much of his work—with a party in her house. Since Stevie Smith (the only poet to whom Enright had written a fan letter) had been a previous recipient of the Medal, and after her account (well known to those who saw Glenda Jackson in the film of her life) of alarming the Queen by talking about 'Death', we must feel relieved that Enright had not yet begun to plan his *Oxford Book of Death* (although, as it was published only two years later, perhaps he had . . .) That Oxford Book, much debated and anguished over by editors and sales staff alike—*who would buy it? to whom could it be given?* (the answer since: everyone)—was proposed by Enright himself, one of his several entirely individual anthologies. David Rawlinson gives us a glimpse of the Johnsonian principles that go into their making.

Is D. J. Enright a poet? This rather perverse question is nevertheless sometimes posed. Clearly all the contributors to this volume find him to be one, though Donald Davie has doubts as to whether *The Terrible Shears* is really 'poetry'. Some readers (and Davie too) feel affronted by an excess of irony—a 'habit of mind that some of us are cursed with'*— especially in poetry. Above all, they feel a lack of aesthetic satisfaction. (It has been said to the present writer, for instance, that Enright should not have attempted *Paradise Illustrated* if he could not emulate the eloquence of Milton. But this criticism is so far from the point of what he was trying to do, that I'm afraid that these two schools of thought may never meet.) In an early essay, 'Literature, Criticism and Belief' (collected in *The Apothecary's Shop*, 1957), Enright quotes Erich Heller as saying 'To make poetry is to think', and although it is not enough to leave this bald statement unqualified here, it would be a fine basis for a defence of Enright as poet.

There are, though, self-imposed limitations to his range: he has not composed formal lyrics, or love-poems—his 'Roman Elegies' remain to be written!—nor poems of nature (though in the early Alexandrian poems, nature is a powerful element). In *Instant Chronicles*,

> Nature was best left
> To the specialists. It reminded him
> Of cross-country runs at school
> In wind and rain.
>
> Then there was Love. Severe girls
> At poetry readings chided him
> For not providing it.
> He left it to the specialists . . .
>   (CP, 317)

When he attempts an affectionate poem (but the poems about his mother are exceptions to this) he becomes awkward and sentimental, as Douglas Dunn mentions. He won't 'curl with metaphors a plain intention'—or, perhaps, treat ironically private feelings. But do we need him to write such poems? The sequences are experimental in their way (as Shirley Chew has shown, in her essay 'Untold Stories'), where omission accomplishes as much as prolonged narrative. Several of the essayists point out stylistic

---

* Donald Davie 'The Image of the Ironist', review of *The Alluring Problem*, in the *Guardian*, 28 November 1988.

weaknesses: a lightness of touch that sometimes falls into mere chattiness; a reluctance to polish; an open-endedness that avoids solutions, or alternatively endings that are too pat; an over-reliance on puns which make one wince rather than grin (on a reading of *Faust*, one can count on a groan when Helen vanishes: ' "Gone to Paris for the weekend," / Mephisto ventured'). His recent poems get terser, they become almost jottings, and nowadays, deliberately, they are often prose. But when he collects his forces, and soars, then it is all the more convincing and disturbing, as in for instance 'Ever-rolling', which ends *Instant Chronicles*.

D. J. Enright has a great many good friends and admirers, as I quickly found out when I sought advice on this book. On behalf of Oxford University Press, I should like to thank the contributors for their enthusiasm and generosity. This book has no ending, for we are now awaiting—as Dennis approaches 70—a new typescript from the poet . . .

JACQUELINE SIMMS
Greenwich, September 1989

I

On *Academic Year*
Alexandria 1947–1950

ANTHONY THWAITE

NOT so many years ago as it sometimes seems, it was possible for literate British persons with qualifications that could hardly be called 'specialist' (and sometimes with very few qualifications at all) to find jobs in universities all over the world as teachers of English Literature. This was before the exacting days of TEFL, TESOP, of ESP and EAP; an innocent epoch, when it would have been unlikely for a British professor to make (or at any rate to make in public) such a bizarre remark as 'literature is useful even in language learning'. Nowadays the display advertisements for English-teaching posts abroad demand a thorough apprenticeship working on the linguistic interface. Experts like Dr Petworth in Malcolm Bradbury's novel *Rates of Exchange* pick up their briefcases and circle the globe carrying with them this 'ideal British product, needing no workers and no work, no assembly lines and no assembly, no spare parts and very little servicing'—the English language.

But until about the mid-1960s, the situation was not like that at all. True, English has been an international language for a long time, but until roughly twenty years ago it was seen to have a close relationship with, if not actually to be embodied in, something called English Literature. In Ankara and Athens, from China to Peru, exported teachers expounded the Great Tradition and the Common Pursuit, the plays of Shakespeare and Shaw, the novels of Dickens and George Eliot, the poems of everyone from Langland to Larkin. Why? One answer has been supplied by D. J. Enright: 'we teach literature because there is as yet no substitute for it.'

In his essay 'The Daffodil Transplanted', from which those words are quoted, D. J. Enright draws on his wide experience of teaching English Literature abroad. He began with three years in Egypt, the setting of his first (of four) novels, *Academic Year*, and went on for varying periods to Japan, Germany, Thailand, and Singapore. These experiences have fed his poems and novels for over forty years: some of them have been relayed more directly but no less entertainingly in one of the sharpest and funniest autobiographies of our time, *Memoirs of a Mendicant Professor*. If we add to these the several books of critical essays Enright has published over the years, we see a consistent, distinct, and remarkable individual. At the end of his *Memoirs*, he calls them 'the animadversions of a disillusioned liberal'; but he continues:

Disillusioned—and yet with no superior illusion in view, and so perhaps not to be accurately called 'disillusioned'. 'Chastened' let us rather say. What you have not deified cannot fail you so utterly. As for 'liberal', I don't think it will ever come to seem a dirty word to me.

That is very much the standpoint of *Academic Year*, written some fifteen years earlier. Enright, born in 1920 into a poor Anglo-Irish family in the Midlands, won his way through scholarships to grammar school and Cambridge. At Cambridge in the late 1930s he was a pupil of F. R. Leavis at Downing College—an experience which neither made him a Leavisite parrot nor turned him into a contemptuous apostate. He contributed to *Scrutiny* while still an undergraduate, which might make one suppose that a conventional and successful domestic academic career lay in front of him. But he has maintained, in an essay in *Conspirators and Poets* (1966), that

for a candidate for home university posts immediately after the war—let alone earlier—to have appeared in the pages of *Scrutiny* was considerably more disadvantageous than to have appeared in no pages at all. Some of us went abroad in the first case . . . simply because foreign universities were less particular or (perhaps through backwardness) less prejudiced against *Scrutiny*'s minor fry.

So in 1947 Enright began his profession of English Literature as a lecturer in what was the Farouk I University, later to be the University of Alexandria. British teachers had long been employed in Egyptian universities. In 1926 Robert Graves was appointed Professor of English Literature at the newly founded Egyptian University in Cairo. He was promised (and received) 'a very high salary' and was assured 'there was little work to do' ('I found that I was expected to give two lectures a week, but the dean soon decided that if the students were ever to dispense with the interpreters they must be given special instruction in French

—which reduced the time for lectures, so that I had only one a week to give. This one was pandemonium'). Graves stayed in Egypt for a year, and was succeeded by Bonamy Dobrée who, presumably treating the place with less arrant contempt, survived three years. Among others in the university roll-call, particularly during the Second World War, were Robin Fedden, Robert Liddell, P. H. Newby, Bernard Spencer, and Terence Tiller.

But the post-war Egypt in which the young Enright arrived was no longer the curiously Bohemian place of temporary intellectual exile conjured up by these names (to which one could add the non-university-based but associated ones of Keith Douglas, Lawrence Durrell, Olivia Manning, R. D. Smith, and several others). These were the last years of Farouk's corrupt and decadent regime. It was a country on the edge of extreme and violent change. In *Academic Year* Enright reflects its mixture of anarchy and repression, nihilism and nerves: riots and rumours of riots and of *coups d'état*, as well as the more customary student strikes. The end of the British Mandate in Palestine in 1948 and the foundation of the state of Israel resulted in the first Arab–Israeli war, and the humiliation, in particular of Egypt, in the subsequent defeat. In 1952, two years after Enright left Egypt, Farouk was forced to abdicate. Though he ostensibly handed over the throne to his infant son, the real power became Neguib and his military council and, behind Neguib, Nasser.

It was a time of apprehension, and of a different kind of scrutiny from that which Enright had experienced at Cambridge. Farouk's Secret Police and so-called Moral Police were everywhere. (Enright casually brings in mention of a member of the latter in the novel.) In an incident which one feels could easily have involved Packet and Bacon in *Academic Year*, but which in fact had to wait to be commemorated in *Memoirs of a Mendicant Professor*, Enright tells of walking along the Corniche with an Irish colleague on their way to take tea with one of the university professors. Enright remarked jokingly to his friend that they were approaching an anti-aircraft gun, newly installed to protect Alexandria against Israeli attacks; so that, although no attempt had been made to camouflage it, they would be well advised not to stare at it as they passed:

We fixed our tactful gaze in front of us, perhaps a little too fixedly, for some bystander, bored with the long Sunday afternoon, conceived the thrilling notion that we might be Jewish spies. Quickly a crowd gathered, and cries of 'Yahudi!', some questioning and some answering, broke the calm of the Corniche.

A policeman having appeared, Enright and his friend were taken to the nearest police station ('a little squalid hell of its own, smelling of urine'), where a lieutenant roared 'When did you swim ashore from that Jewish ship?' Fortunately the interrogation was curtailed by the chance intervention of a coffee-drinking chum of the assembled policemen. He turned out to be a clerk in the university administration who recognized Enright and vouched for his identity and respectability, 'and everybody smiled and exclaimed and congratulated everybody else':

I suggested hesitantly that since the police had made us late for our appointment, they might like to stand us a taxi. That was the funniest joke of all. We stumbled past the prostrate women and the quarrelling policemen with laughter exploding at our heels. Drama had turned to comedy, and that was the next best thing on a boring Sunday at the police station.

In *Academic Year*, drama often turns to comedy, and vice versa. When the novel was first published in 1955, it was greeted with genial praise, but almost wholly as a comedy, if not actually a farce. It followed close on the heels of John Wain's *Hurry On Down* and Kingsley Amis's *Lucky Jim*, and it was in their terms that it was praised: the *Daily Telegraph*, in fact, called it 'an Alexandrian *Lucky Jim*'. The *Star* thought it 'should give the right-minded reader many a laugh and not a few reminiscent chuckles later on'. The *New Statesman* called it 'splendidly seedy'—'a phrase which' (thinks Packet, in the opening pages of *Academic Year*'s sequel, *Heaven Knows Where*) 'might be taken to connote one shelf above the consciously pornographic'. Certainly it is a great deal funnier than that other, vaster literary memorial to Alexandria of modern times, Durrell's *Alexandria Quartet*, the first volume of which (*Justine*) appeared two years after *Academic Year*, in 1957. Nothing could be more different than these two poets' treatment of the city and its inhabitants. But rereading Enright's novel almost thirty years after its first appearance, I found that my memory had played tricks. I too had remembered it as much more of a comic turn, much more a slice of farcical picaresque, than in fact is the case. I had forgotten how, among the jokes and the flippant observations, the book has a strong vein of melancholy, disgust, and even tragedy.

Its three central performers can be seen (as William Walsh has pointed out)* as embodiments of 'the experienced, the ardent, and the intolerant in the English character, and present a kind of English solidity in the face of the aspiring and impalpable Egyptian sensibility'. There is Bacon, an oldish lecturer at the university, 'that Egyptianised *pagliaccio*', as he is described, an affable and boozy cynic; Packet, a younger lecturer and in some sense Enright's mouthpiece (though it is Bacon who, in Chapter 5, delivers what is in fact an early Enright poem, 'Children, Beggars and Schoolteachers'); and there is Brett, a young prig newly arrived and employed at the Cultural Centre.

In the course of the academic year Packet has his hopeless affair with Sylvie, the kind but worldly-wise westernized Syrian; Brett witnesses a small boy shot dead in the act of looting a shop; Bacon, threatened by ruffians pretending to avenge a family debt of honour, is killed with a knife. This is not really the stuff of comedy, certainly not of farce. The apophthegms and definitions are witty and sardonic, but they are not lightweight: 'The terror of lawlessness had been succeeded by the terrorism of law. And the latter was more dangerous in a way, because it was more organised and better armed and it had less of a sense of humour.' And perhaps more pervasive than any of the characters is the city itself, that 'vast account book: debit and credit side by side, and sizeable sums in each column', the city which 'itself was a colossal lie', grandiosely ennobled with the name of its great founder, and by the late 1940s a polyglot sprawl of Greeks, French, Jews, Italians, ranged against the Egyptians and all the other Levantine mixtures of races and creeds.

Of course it *is* a book full of hilarious passages and persons as well. Anyone who has ever taught in a Middle Eastern university will recognize with delight the duplicating machine for the printing of examination papers installed in the lavatory, and the stunningly unmarkable answers written during the feverish exam rituals ('Dickens' father was not successful in his marriage and he had ten children'). Enright's command of Arab student English

---

* D. J. Enright: *Poet of Humanism*, Cambridge University Press, 1974.

(beseeching, charming, ingratiating, insolent) is superb: 'We all honour you, sir, you are our teacher. But we cannot work today—it is Down with Britain day, if you will excuse it, sir.' One wouldn't want to do without Sylvie's effusively Frenchified relative, Madame Nader—or her dog.

But alongside the fun and frolics there is much of what the Japanese have come to call the Enrightenment: the sense that 'There had been too much politics over the past twenty years: we had almost forgotten what it was to be merely human.' The sheer precariousness of life is the novel's uninsisted centre, 'made up of short violences and short calms, brief sorrows and brief joys'. One is grateful that, things being what they were and his background being what it was, Enright chose in 1947 to embark on his career as peripatetic teacher of literature. His learning and his liberality of spirit made him a good teacher; his acute and mordant observation and wit made him a good poet and novelist; his restlessness—and his apparent capacity for putting his foot into official quagmires—made him keep moving on. Egypt was a fortunate first place for his gifts. At one point in *Academic Year*, the avuncular Bacon suggests to Packet that he 'could write a novel about our Alexandrian revels. Why not make some use of those crammed notebooks?' Young Packet / Enright did; and the result was and is a modern classic not just of mendicant professorialism or campus japes slightly west of Suez, but of surprising sharpness and seriousness.

Enright's Japan
1953–1956

RUSSELL GREENWOOD

'IN the early Fifties we were the only / Foreign family in the hamlet of Okamoto', wrote D. J. Enright years later, in *The Terrible Shears*. He added that 'the natives were very kind to us'. Deservedly so, for the kindness was reciprocal, and Dennis, his French wife, and their diminutive daughter were most welcome strangers in Okamoto / Sumiyoshi, still relatively rural areas on the outer fringes of the city and port of Kobe.

They were lucky to have chosen Kobe as their centre for activity. Whereas Tokyo (the Dai-Wen) so dominates its satellite cities, Kobe is simply one of three points in the Kansai triangle. Osaka is pre-eminently the bustling centre of big business and banking. 'Making any money?' is the traditional greeting, 'couldn't be worse!' the standard reply. Kyoto, with delectable Nara nearby as an unexpected bonus, is the decorous pillar of culture and learning, almost as arcane now as it was in the Heian period, the days of Sei Shonagon and Murasaki Shikibu. Kobe, though by no means lacking in a history of its own, is the newcomer of the three, cosmopolitan even in the Fifties, jaunty, and a little given to excess, as if it had heard one too many mariner's tales.

By rail at least, all these cities are so close and accessible that an intrepid traveller—the Enrights were intrepid—may breakfast in Kobe, take lunch in Osaka, and dine in Kyoto. It would just be possible, with a bit of Pelion on Ossa, to include a cucumber-sandwich tea in Nara in the nineteenth-century lounge of the Nara Hotel's old wing, where the ghosts of such British Japanophiles as Sir Ernest Satow or Sir George Sansom may be summoned up without undue alarm.

The speed of modern travel and the sense of antiquity, the solemn dignity of a Kyoto temple garden and the garishness of the advertisement displays immediately surrounding the temple precincts, produce a perpetual sense of contrast in Japan. The country is always a paradox, bewildering to poet and to mute inglorious alike. The medal, like the Queen's Gold Medal for Poetry, awarded to Enright in 1981, displays the remarkable reverse. After nearly four decades of absence, would the Enrights recognize Japan today? The answer, predictably, can only be Yes and No.

No, because Kobe's skyline, always impressive, has seen many a change, with vast new buildings, from the admirable, through the merely grandiose, to the distinctly grotty. Okamoto is today a smart and expensive suburb, with blocks of apartments edging their way up the hillsides. In a uniquely Japanese fit of zeal, they even sliced the top off a minor mountain, though the twin peaks of Rokko San and Maya San remain comparatively undisturbed. The surplus earth has been transported to the sea by conveyor-belt and bogie, then redistributed to provide the foundations for a high-tech container port, sports-and-leisure complex, plus a luxury hotel called Portopia. Pelion off Ossa, in this case. Romans will be relieved to note that all this was not accomplished in one day.

Yes, some things would remain recognizable, since Japan is a very mountainous, labyrinthine country, where comic little railways clunk their way up and down the hills. The ruling party needs the farmers' votes, so no one has ever dared to do a Beeching on Japanese railways, and loss-making lines can still shake you past the rice terraces, 'the pasteboard houses and the plywood schools', which Enright saw in 1953 as a Busybody under a Cherry Tree. They may be taking you to a sophisticated terminus like Arima hot springs or, if you are prepared to travel hopefully, you may still in the Nineties find yourself alongside peasants, produce, even poultry and piglets, in a manner and milieu more reminiscent of a stopping train in Southern Thailand.

Distance may lend enchantment to the view, but, to view Enright's Japan in 1953, a pair of powerful binoculars is required. Japan was an early stage on a journey which had already taken in Cambridge, extra-mural Birmingham, and, in between, exotic Alexandria with shades of Cavafy. With Berlin, Bangkok, and an epic stint in Singapore ahead, it was to be a lengthy journey, with some bumpy take-offs and landings, with occasional turbulence in the air. It must have been a relief eventually to sink into the swivel-chair at Chatto & Windus vacated by C. Day Lewis. My only object in this biographizing is to wonder how far the Japanese experience coloured the subsequent product, especially the twelve years or so in South-East Asia. There are few echoes of Egypt in the poems of the Japanese period, but there seems to me— with hindsight, perhaps—quite a lot of Japan's influence in the later work. The Japanese experience, except to the insensitive or actively hostile, tends to be a lasting one.

Since the Enright family were the only foreigners in Okamoto, I should perhaps declare my interest, as I was the only long-nosed foreign devil in the adjacent village of Mikage (Honourable Shade), just one stop down the line. We became friends, and since then it has been a pleasure and privilege to dwell in the 'honourable shade' of the Enrights in more countries than one. Kōnan University lies in the neighbourhood of these hamlets, far from Elsinore. Enright was appointed Visiting Professor, a title bestowed somewhat indiscriminately by the Japanese, but infinitely preferable to 'Distinguished Professor'—an Enright abomination.

Kōnan is one of the best private universities in Japan, though Keio and Waseda, Tokyo's leading (and rival) private universities might be tempted to dispute the claim. This type of university often has many mansions and many manifestations. Kōnan, for example, has a senior boys' high school which it likes to call 'the Eton of Japan'. The rivals for this distinction are so formidably vociferous that the Battle of Waterloo could well have passed unnoticed on their playing fields. Still, Kōnan was ambitious enough to invite D. J. Enright, possibly with outside support, for in those days Japan was poor (newly deserving poor) and we were allegedly prosperous. Extracting the binoculars again, one can see through the mist Austin A40s and Hillman Minxes shipped sectionally to Yokohama for the Japanese to complete a screwdriver operation. They were not too bad on buses and light pick-up trucks (dubbed 'bata bata') but had not yet mastered the art of inventing, producing, much less mass-producing, a serious saloon car.

Accommodation appropriate to a lower-case distinguished Professor from Oxbridge was in short supply (it still is today). So the Enrights moved in initially with one of Kōnan's trustees. They were really rich, perhaps one of the reasons for Enright's early awareness of the contrasts of wealth as in 'Happy New Year', when:

. . . I met a banker weeping through his smiles
upon that hectic morn.

Omedetō, he told me while the saké bubbled on his lips.
His frock-coat trembled in its new and yearly bliss.
'A hard year for Japan' . . .

and, walking away from the 'bright new house':

> . . . my head was full of yen, of falling yen.
> I saw the others, with their empty pockets,
> Merry on the old year's dregs, their mouths distilled a warm
>   amen!

(CP, 19–20)

Enright's host was Chobei Takeda, the Chairman of Takeda
Pharmaceuticals, the Mr Boots of Japan. An orchid-lover, he
too had been at Cambridge before the war, and, as the sixth
generation of his family firm, had heard the chimes at midnight.
If Takeda was Dennis's first Lord High Executioner, then Yujiro
Iwai was Lord High Everything Else. He was Chairman of what
is now Nissho–Iwai, one of Japan's Big Six trading companies.
He ruled the Japan–British Society with an iron hand in a not-
so-velvet glove. By a great coincidence, he (too) had been at
Emmanuel College, Cambridge, contemporary with the then
British Consul-General, a dear, dour man, whom Iwai once
described to me as 'a bit of a poet, like Enright'. Iwai took to the
Enrights and introduced them to *fugu*, the blow-fish, delicious
but lethal if ill-prepared. A number of people die of *fugu* poisoning
every year; some are said to play Russian roulette with its
poisonous elements. Foreign professors, expensively imported,
are not permitted to die thus, company chairmen even less so. A
fairly safe way of embarking on *fugu* is through an invitation from
the Chairman of a major Japanese company. Roman Emperors
took precautionary measures not dissimilar in nature.

If I have elaborated on these tycoons (one of the few English
words indisputably derived from the Japanese), it is because
I think they were important to Enright. They at least had a
modicum of shared educational experience. They were tough, but
kindly men. They were helping to resurrect Japan from an abject
post-war poverty to a living competence, towards a global respect
for their commercial integrity and, after their deaths, to a national
GDP beyond their wildest expectations.

On the academic side, though there were always shining exceptions, there was little to learn from the average *sensei**. They were then ill paid, ill housed, often ill clad and, though they retained their special status, they found it hard to command general respect. Books in foreign languages were in short supply, but were occasionally made available through the ministrations of a benign and Midas-like United States government. I recall one particular occasion when a number of Japanese academics benefited from an unusual concatenation of circumstances. The monstrous Senator McCarthy sent his henchmen, Cohn and Schine, round the USIS libraries of Japan, the consequence of which was the banning of books by authors other than US citizens. Thus quantities of heavily labelled volumes of Shakespeare, Bunyan, Wordsworth, down to Keynes and Orwell, found their way into Japanese university libraries. The USIS officials stopped well short of burning the books—though I encountered one or two of them who would gladly have consigned Messrs Cohn and Schine to the flames.

Enright was encouraged towards Kyoto, to some extent by the British Council who were then keen to expand in that desirable direction. Not that it normally takes much persuasion to move in the direction of Kyoto. (And, the sooner it is said the better, D. J. Enright does take kindly to being directed by officials. Quite rightly so, but that was later, and in another country.) For a time he kept an eye on the books that later became the basis of the Council's library, and gave a weekly lecture in Kyoto. There were more sensitive teachers to be found in unbombed Kyoto: to have seen the city, as I did, just after the end of the war and to have compared it with the devastation elsewhere in Japan was a revelation of a chastening, even chilling, nature. Enright seemed to find it a 'grey city':

> A pallid grace invests the gliding cars.
> The Kamo keeps its decent way, not opulent nor bare.
> The last light waves a fading hand. Now fiercer seasons
>   start like neon in the little bars.

(CP, 30)

* '*Sensei*. A magic word, and yet very equivocal. *Sensei* means "teacher" plus "scholar" plus "beloved master"; it means intellect, learning, culture, taste . . . Yet it also means "those who can't do, teach", a reciter of old lecture notes . . .' (DJE, *The World of Dew*, 24).

Probably the most distinguished of these teachers was the late Bunshō Jugaku, very much a scholar of the old school, but also a person whose pallid grace invested the word *sensei* with greater dignity than the more raucous *shacho* (company chairman) could ever command. He was expert in many fields, but especially on Blake and Dante. When I visited Professor Jugaku, then housebound, in the later Seventies, he recalled Enright with visible pleasure as a good, kind, and generous man. Another jovial influence of a more voluptuous nature was Osaka's Prefectural Librarian, Nakamura, translator of some of Winston Churchill's works. Though Osaka was his home, he gravitated quite naturally to Kyoto and occasionally entertained his favourite foreigners in Ponto-chō or Gion, the original geisha quarters of Heian Japan. These riverside districts, now hideously marred by boutiques or even jazz bars, had a gentle grace of their own. They were, at their best, inaccessible to a foreigner except as the accompanied guest of a Japanese *habitué*. There perhaps, 'the Kamo keeps its decent way' in a manner of speaking—or possibly poetic licence is justifiable in the licensed quarters.

Enright's Japan was not confined to the Kansai. Even then, Tokyo beckoned. It was, after all, 'that Eastern capital', as an elderly aristocratic lady from Kyoto ('the capital capital') once described it to me disparagingly. The so-called bullet train now takes some three hours from Osaka to Tokyo. In those days, the stately express departed from Osaka's Umeda Station at precisely 9 a.m. and reached Tokyo at precisely 5 p.m., the white-gloved station masters being at hand both on departure and arrival. They usually looked at their watches, approvingly.

Enright had friends in Tokyo: for instance, Bill and Helen MacAlpine, a cheerful and curiously ubiquitous couple who were equally at home in Dylan Thomas's Soho as they were in the bar of the Strand Hotel, Rangoon. Another lively soul was the late Kenichi Yoshida, critic, belle-lettrist, saké-lover, who had been an undergraduate briefly but, by his own admission, ingloriously, at King's, Cambridge (again!); one cross that Kenichi managed to bear fairly lightly was that his father throughout that period was Japan's Prime Minister.

Some of the Tokyo experiences emerged in later poems, in *Addictions* (1962), for instance, where the poem 'In Memoriam' simultaneously observes a live elephant on the roof of the

Takashimaya Department Store and a dying Englishman, who had been Takashimaya's Father Christmas:

> He would have died anywhere.
> And he lived his last year in Japan, loved by a
> Japanese orphan, teaching her the rudiments of
> Happiness, and (without certificate) teaching
> Japanese students.
>
> (CP, 49–50)

But Tokyo by stately railway train was a long way from Okamoto. Social life in Kobe was less rarefied, and evening relaxation most easily obtained by taking the prestigious Hankyu Line from Okamoto to Kobe's Sannomiya Station. Three railway companies sent their trains on separate tracks, competitive, relentless, and parallel, between Osaka and Kobe, to where, much lower down the scale, indeed under the tracks of the oft-despised National Railway, stood or crouched the Bar Canna, alas no more. A cheerful and understanding Mama San, assisted by three girls (Akiko, Sumiko, Chiyako), entertained from behind their Stand Bar, as they were then called: they stood behind the bar, you sat in front. And chatted and drank a fair amount of bottled beer which might cost the guest £2 or £3 a session (now tenfold for its approximate equivalent). We often went there, virtually the only foreigners, but apparently welcome. Especially Dennis's wife, who often accompanied us, and who personified the security of marriage and to the girls the opportunity to catch a rare glimpse of European womanhood, surely a dream of French luxury (or lingerie) and fine living.

Enright wrote of all this in *The World of Dew*, and concluded that there was less 'viciousness' in Japan than could be found 'in Piccadilly or Place Pigalle'. It was the world of Miss Moth rather than Madam Butterfly. Their names, if not their attributes, appear in their poems: Akiko, 'she shall be glorified, if any are'; and Sumiko:

> So pour the small beer, Sumichan. And girls
>   permit yourselves a hiccup, the thunder
> Of humanity. The helpless alley is held by
>   sleeping beggars under
> Their stirring beards . . .
>
> (CP, 20–1)

The objects of Enright's compassion, in and out of the Canna, were there for all to see. The girls were poor but honest, the beggars still poorer and with fewer hopes. All were a long way (ten minutes by taxi at 11 p.m.) from Chobei Takeda's orchids and his pharmaceutical products, on which they had to rely to survive. If they could afford to survive was the message of the plaintive poems. Bleak, but not quite so annihilating as 'Hiroshima', whose citizens might have wished for something lasting, 'like a wooden box'.

For Enright as teacher there must have been grounds for frustration as well as compassion. The average Japanese university student, though often endearingly loyal, is not very articulate in any language. Nor is he ('she' more often is) noticeably diligent, since the university tends to be looked upon as a four-year breathing-space (not necessarily an unworthy assumption) between the examination hell which has preceded it and the highly competitive business world which is to follow. So a well-delivered lecture is apt to be received with deafening silence, a plea for co-operative questions with blank dismay; most amiable jokes, except straight banana-skin, drop with a dull thud. Sometimes a similar sense of the dead hand can be felt in relations with academic colleagues, as if the new broom, once swept clean, can now be discarded. The foreign lecturer tends to search his conscience and ask 'where did I go wrong?'

> It is alleged
> An empty saké bottle in your company was seen . . .
>   (CP, 27)

But he need not worry, any more than Hokusai's mad poet need worry. The tap turned off will suddenly turn on again, often with some gesture as welcome as it is unexpected. In Enright's case, it seemed to at least one observer that his wit, good humour, and lively sense of the ridiculous was always at hand to provide a more than adequate antidote to frustrations of this kind.

Aside from the academic world, there must have been many problems in maintaining a family home in nether Kansai in the early Fifties. True, a live-in cook, nanny-cum-maid-of-all-work was an eminently feasible proposition and some combination of this arrangement represented a necessity for the Enrights. The near-prose poem 'A Poor Little Lonely Child' perfectly depicts the domestic scene. The parents gad about, the mother lectures in French, marks examination papers, the father lectures on good literature and takes refuge at home in bad language. It is a nightmare of a Cultural Festival to which the parents are bidden: the description does justice to the inanities that the Japanese are occasionally capable of perpetrating. On their return home, the child greets her parents with the pertinent observations of a 4-year-old on a new and arty Japanese plate:

> 'That is a good plate. I do not like it, now. Because I
> do not like the colours, now. But that is a good plate.
> And I shall like it when I am bigger.'

(CP, 24–5)

How right and reassuring. Said with all the aplomb of her four years, with quite a bit of schooling already behind her, including personal attention from the 'Head Monster', as she calls him in 'Blue Umbrellas'.

Verbal sallies have always intrigued Enright, who in his essays has given a measure of praise to the pun, and has mused outrageously on his Swedish typewriter called FACIT. In Japan, there was ample scope for this, dextrously when the Japanese were employing their own language, less so when the medium was the English language. Every self-respecting salary-man in Japan, even the teacher-poet, requires a seal or 'chop' for the transaction of official business. In Japanese *kanji*, Enright acquired an impressive seal, the three characters of which, to his delight, read 'EN-RAI-TO' or 'Monkey comes to town'. Madeleine had to be similarly equipped, for Western wives are often accommodated in areas where most Japanese wives would fear to tread (though they are frequently the real guardians of the family finances). She was rewarded with a seal differing only in the initial character, and became 'Swallow comes to town'.

In English the situation is more precarious. As is well known, Japanese has no letter 'l', so the capital city of the United Kingdom is 'Rondon'. It is peculiarly contagious, and I once found myself in temporary agreement with a student who said 'O for orange, R for remon.' But the sagacious Japanese *sensei* who has regaled his students with ponderous jokes about 'Words'worth' over-compensates. Aware of his language's consonantal deficiencies and recognizing that 'r' is a sop to Cerberus, he will in all seriousness address his letters to 'Professor D. J. Enlight', with its clear intimations of immortality.

For over a century now, foreign teachers of English have visited Japan. Today there are thousands, varying from the refreshingly youthful and idealistic, to the highly skilled language teachers and not forgetting the unwashed sub-culture ('Come, come, Baby. English lessons'—a notice I once pointed out to Enright, mentioned in *The World of Dew*). But there were some notable characters in the distant past. Lafcadio Hearn can scarcely be included amongst the British contingent, for he was such a mixture from the cradle to the grave, ending his days as Yakumo Koizumi, his wife's maiden name, revered but rootless. Later there were many others. Unlike today when it is highly profitable to come to Japan to teach, it was in pre-war days fashionably eccentric. After all, Part III of *Gulliver's Travels* was entitled 'A voyage of Laputa, Balnibarbi, Luggnagg, Glubbdubdrib and Japan'. Writers of the stature of Peter Quennell, William Plomer, and William Empson went out to Japan and made their temporary marks, but scarcely a ripple remains. The exception is the self-effacing Edmund Blunden (later, as Enright acknowledged in his *World of Dew*, the 'Honourable Mr Middleman' who introduced him to Kōnan University). Hearn came and stayed forever. Of the others, only Blunden returned. The Professor at Tokyo University, 1924–7, became the Cultural Attaché at the UK Liaison Mission (i.e. Embassy) 1948–50. I recall a slightly exasperated American diplomat saying at the time, 'We put USIS officers all over the country. You do it with one Blunden.' He certainly scattered his image through the land in the way of *ad hoc* verses. There seem to be a proliferation of Blunden originals at Senior High Schools and the like in most quarters of Japan. Even the one genuine English pub in Kobe (now completely Japanese-owned, but 'lovingly preserved', as Pevsner would say) is honoured with a Blunden sonnet, ending like a wounded, though non-Alexandrine, snake: 'with the King's Arms proud over it'.

How far, then, did D. J. Enright enlighten the Japanese scene in the Fifties? Probably far more than he ever imagined ('The best fruits of a good teacher's work are those he is never likely to see', observed the late scholar-educationalist, Sir Richard Livingstone, a shade sententiously). But his praises are still sung there, by acquaintances ranging from very elderly professor, ex-University of Hiroshima, to ex-student of Kyoto University, now himself a professor in Nara, and visiting professor at Kōnan Women's University. Which is significant for one who left so long ago, and never came back. I have often wanted to ask Dennis whether his motto, unconsciously albeit, might not be:

> The Moving Finger writes; and, having writ,
> Moves on . . .

The Mendicant Professor:

A Self-confessed Liberal in Singapore, 1960–1970

KOH TAI ANN

IN 1984, when—some fourteen years after his departure from Singapore—D. J. Enright was mentioned in the British and international press as a possible (if reluctant) choice for the British Poet Laureateship, the *Straits Times* commissioned a special feature on him, believing rightly that there was still enough interest among Singaporeans. In my piece, I recalled:

Part of Enright's greatness as a teacher lay in his regard for what people intrinsically are. The concluding line of his poem 'A Chasm in the Classroom', 'I beg to differ, not dissuade', reveals this respect, as much as his declaration once, with reference to his students, 'I had no wish . . . to take into my hands the springs of their being. They are neither tap-water nor plasticine.'

A second article in the same paper asked other former students to record their views and memories of him. Not surprisingly, he was recalled with affection for his kindness and generosity, and with admiration for the way he taught literature, or rather, the reading, critical study, and enjoyment of it. One student recalled that he 'had a reputation for conducting the most "listenable" lectures, which even non-English students attended'.

Yet Enright was known at the time, and is generally remembered in Singapore, in connection with the so-called 'Enright Affair'. He has recorded this in detail in his own *Memoirs*, but it may be useful at this remove, thirty years later, to set the affair in a wider context. When he gave his inaugural lecture as the Johore Professor of English at the then University of Malaya (since 1961, the University of Singapore), it was selectively quoted in the paper the next day. Enright's lecture was entitled 'Robert Graves and the Decline of Modernism', but it was his preliminary comments reflecting on the cultural policies of the newly elected Singapore government that made headline news, and provoked a strong government reaction. Enright had said that culture was built 'by people listening to music and composing it, reading books and writing them, looking at pictures and painting them, and observing life and living it'; Singapore and Malaya should, he said, 'remain culturally *open*'. More controversially, he said that to institute 'a sarong-culture, complete with pantun competitions and so forth' would be as ridiculous as 'to bring back the Maypole and the Morris dancers in England just because the present monarch happens to be called Elizabeth.'

The Acting Minister for Law and Labour (whom Enright believed was given this role 'because he was the one Malay minister at the time') summoned him to his office, and threatened to withdraw his work permit. In an abusive open letter, evidently penned by the Minister of Culture who was present at the interview, Enright was called (among other things) a 'mendicant professor'—an epithet which he has, with characteristic wit, turned to his advantage in the ambiguous title of his *Memoirs*.* The Students' Union backed Enright, on the grounds of 'academic freedom'— but if it had not been for the shrewd political instincts of the Prime Minister Lee Kuan Yew, who genially addressed the Students' Union and effectively closed the matter, things might have turned out worse. As it was, the Affair rankled for years. Enright stayed on, but when in July 1966 his name was once again invoked against alleged government infringement of 'university autonomy and academic freedom', he was moved to write to the press rejecting the 'symbolic status' his name had by then achieved. Indeed, he wrote, he had become 'sick and tired of it', as if he had 'done nothing either before or since to justify his existence' other than to be involved in 'that rather ludicrous business'.

The Affair certainly had its ludicrous aspects, which are related with amusement in Enright's *Memoirs*, not least thanks to his offhand or satirical comments about what he, as a self-confessed Western liberal, regarded as absurd, but what others (as always in such circumstances) held with passionate intensity. His apparently high-handed tone seems to have touched raw nerves, and however unwittingly, triggered off an over-reaction from a politically

* *Memoirs of a Mendicant Professor*, Chatto & Windus, 1969; reprint by Carcanet Press, 1990. In Chap. 15 Enright outlines the situation in which he found himself, and quotes in full the partial quoting from the *Straits Times*; the open letter; and ensuing correspondence. (Ed.)

insecure government, sensitive to racial tensions in a pluralist society. The policies that Enright questioned were intended to defuse those very tensions by encouraging the use of Malay as the 'national language' (Malay, as opposed to English or Chinese), and the creation of a Malayan cultural identity. The Singapore government seems to have seized on the occasion as a nationalistic opportunity to avenge past colonial humiliations, and to show the expatriate community, Singaporeans, and the world who was paying the piper (and, indeed, the professor), and wearing the boots.

C. M. Turnbull, a historian who once taught at the University of Singapore, gives a good idea of the political atmosphere of the time. This to some extent explains how easy it was for Enright, in his (to use the description of the British journalist, Alex Josey) 'political innocence' to stumble into the 'heat and dust of the political arena' — as Prime Minister Lee was to put it. In her *History of Singapore 1819–1975*, Professor Turnbull observes:

The PAP [left-wing People's Action Party]'s clear victory at the polls struck chill in the hearts of businessmen, and property owners, especially expatriates who regarded the election as the prelude to irresponsible and vindictive government and ultimately to communism. Up to that time the party's activities had on the surface been almost entirely disruptive, and Lee Kuan Yew's group had given open encouragement to the extravagant demands of the extremist wing. The storms in the legislative assembly, the pandemonium at City Hall, the anti-capitalist tirades, the strikes and demonstrations which had troubled Singapore in the past four years had already undermined the confidence of businessmen . . . The new regime launched an attack upon Western culture and pressed heavily upon the hitherto privileged English-educated middle class. Six thousand civil servants suffered a cut in allowances and were drafted into carrying out 'voluntary' manual work on Sundays. Western films and magazines which were held to have a corrupting influence or to belittle Asian culture were banned.

The newly-arrived Englishman could not be expected to know that the moderate English-educated wing of the PAP was involved in a mortal struggle for control of the party, and hence of Singapore. Its leaders believed that the government had to react harshly to the white man's criticism of an Asian or Malay culture if it was to retain its credibility within the PAP. Enright's liberal suggestions that such things as pop music, juke-boxes, brothels, and pornography should be left to individual choice and not to legislation, was, in the circumstances, provocative. The tone of his comments, speaking *ex cathedra*, as it were, from the prestigious and only English-speaking university, and the tenor of the London *Times* editorial in his support, revealed an insensitivity to the special circumstances of newly decolonized nations. Thus, the London *Times*, in its editorial of 26 November 1960, could opine:

'Surely, Singapore should welcome the comments of someone whose position, if not his citizenship, gives him an unquestionable status in Singapore's cultural life'; [that while] 'on the face of it, the aim of asserting a national culture is understandable, to legislate for a new culture is simply to misunderstand the nature of any culture . . . The choice of an official language [i.e. Malay] may impose itself and political factors such as a federation with Malaya may influence the choice . . . But too much talk of a "Malayan culture" will prove itself as so much hot air.'

This is lordly stuff!

The opposite viewpoint was put by Professor T. H. Silcock (a former Head of the Economics Department at the University of Malaya), who showed a shrewder political and historical sense when he pointed out in a letter to the London *Times* that both Enright and the Singapore government were victims of circumstances created by past British imperial policies.

Thus it was that Enright soon discovered that 'in the new countries everything from the beginning has been "political".' In a multicultural, multiracial society like Singapore's, which had recently gone through a period of great instability, with two more major racial riots to come during Enright's stay, culture is a political matter; and among the most political of matters after culture, is language. In fact, Singapore was to separate from Malaysia in 1965, after only two years of Federation. The Chinese University of Nanyang was closed and merged in 1980 with the University of Singapore to form the present National University of Singapore, and in 1987 English became the sole medium of instruction in schools and tertiary institutions.

To return to the somewhat shattered ivory tower of the English department—from which Enright was eventually to resign, in less than happy circumstances. With the benefit of hindsight, one can see that his resignation ten years later over his disagreement with the direction the Department should be taking, was already foreshadowed in the Affair. Enright tells us in his *Memoirs* how for a long time afterwards he was to feel 'the faint odium . . . of official disfavour attaching to the Professor of English'; and the 'odium' clung too, to the English Department, since in most eyes it came to be regarded as virtually synonymous with Enright and his emphasis on the study of English literature and not the English language.

Enright's belief in the unquestionable moral value of English literature (and so in the role of the teacher of literature, as opposed to the more functional teaching of the English language) ensured he would eventually be out of step with the government's policies, which by now more closely dictated those of the university. His position on literature and language teaching is clearly indicated in the conclusion he reached after attending his first-ever international conference in 1966. The theme was 'English as a University Subject in the West Pacific': Enright was quick to note 'the ominous cleft between teachers of literature . . . and experts on linguistics, and that mutual hostility which only the linguisticians, insolently charitable in the knowledge of approaching victory, deny the existence of.' These observations were recorded in the *Memoirs*, in the last chapter, 'Apology for Mendicancy', which is actually an unapologetic defence and justification of his profession:

The teacher of literature is inevitably something of a missionary. . . . The language teacher on the other hand is a technician, he is concerned with words, but not with their meaning. The literature teacher actually wants his pupils to be changed by literature; the language teacher merely wants them to be made more efficient members of a given society, to fit in more neatly, to be more efficient citizens. . . .

The growing ascendancy of language teaching (the provision of means) over literature teaching (the examination of ends) is only another instance of what seems to be happening all over the world. We have lost faith in ourselves, without acquiring humility; the measure of our self-contempt is that before long we may be finally content to be 'realistic'. . . . As a liberal and a teacher of literature, I sometimes suspect that, rather unfairly, I am a member of two dying races.

It seems to me that these (in his own words) 'old-fashioned' convictions may help to explain Enright's 'political innocence', his being out of step with the 'realities', and his often edgy relationship with the authorities in Singapore, his letter of resignation ever ready in his shirt pocket. That Enright, a self-confessed 'non-political man', 'high-minded poet' (this more ironically perhaps), and 'liberal' intellectual and teacher, should none the less find himself in the midst of the political arena is due to his coming from another historical context, that has also to do with Empire. A combination of pragmatism (the Empire needed middle-echelon, English-trained civil servants and a supportive, English-educated native middle class), national pride (we recall Lord Macaulay's notorious Minute of 1835 about the superiority of European over Asian literature), and altruism (embodied in British missionaries, teachers, doctors, nurses, and others), resulted in the British exporting to the colonies (among other things) the university as an institution, their language and literature, and more potently, an *idea* of each. In Enright's case the idea of the university and of literature seems to have reached him through Cambridge, and particularly through F. R. Leavis, who was his tutor there.

Leavis saw in Britain's culture a potentially exemplary and inspirational force, a force the nurturer and guardian of which was the university.* He himself came out of an Arnoldian tradition which made of English literature a sort of 'poor man's classics', and assigned to it a civilizing and socializing function in education. On one level, the teaching of literature in the schools was implicitly believed to be a means of acculturating the working class, of forming and refining its sensibility; at another level, at the level of tertiary education, as 'Queen of the Humanities' it helped to conserve and propagate 'humane values'.

Through the constitution of English as a subject in British, and then colonial, universities, and through colonial teachers of literature, the sensibility or tastes of students who were to become the readers, writers, or critics in post-colonial societies were to be effectively formed in this school. To talk of 'tradition', and 'judgement', even to conceive of a canon with some sense of an ordering tradition, is to testify to having been formed by Leavisite criticism and to having acquired a certain outlook on what constitutes literature, literary studies, and 'the critical function'.

* See *Education and the University*, 1943.

When Enright came out East, the dream of Empire was already (as he wryly notes in a poem), 'ruined castles in a vanished Spain'. Another dream had begun: 'The dream of self-determination, / Self-empire'. Coming lately, the poet Enright, who would be 'a sort of Virgil', must be content with only 'Shabby Imperial Dreams':

> I confess with shame
> That I have had such dreams.
> My only plea is,
> I was sleeping at the time—
>   (CP, 84–5)

Unlike the countries of the Indian subcontinent, 'self-empire' came much later to Britain's South-East Asian possessions. Even when Enright first applied for the Johore Chair of English in 1958*, Singapore was still a colony, and the University very much a colonial institution based on the British model. The previous incumbent would have arrived very much the colonial officer to head a department in a university dominated by British or British-trained and appointed expatriates, and he would have been deferred to as a member of the Establishment. But by the time, two years later, when Enright reapplied, as we have seen, significant changes had taken place in the country, and the university was coming under closer political control.

Today the situation of English literature and the language in post-colonial societies such as Singapore's, and the 'realities', are authoritatively described by Enright's successor, Edwin Thumboo, a Singapore poet and literary critic. In 'English Literature in a Global Context', a paper presented at a seminar on 'Progress in English Studies' held in London in 1984 to celebrate the Fiftieth Anniversary of the British Council, Professor Thumboo declared, that in post-colonial societies, even though our primary interest is in literature, we cannot overlook the importance of

the English language as a discipline, particularly if it emphasises both a knowledge of the language and the development of active linguistic skills. Levels of response to the literature correlate fairly accurately with levels of competence in the language. Whether the study of English

---

* See DJE, *Memoirs of a Mendicant Professor*, 115.

literature thrives or declines is directly related to the size of the English language base. . . . In a situation of linguistic and cultural pluralism, standards invariably declined with fairly obvious consequences for the study of literature in a variety that is standard, metropolitan.

And with the survival of English in post-colonial Singapore as the *lingua franca* of continued economic development and the creation of a common cultural identity transcending divisive loyalties to race, religion, and ethnic cultures, it may seem ironic that even the views expressed in Enright's inaugural lecture, such as that Singapore should remain 'culturally open' and the government less authoritarian in its cultural policies, are now commonplace.*

Beyond ideology, history, and politics, and beyond nationalistic sensitivities, and where it counts in human terms, Enright is, and will be, best remembered as a teacher, for his commitment to literature and to his students. Certainly, in his teaching and his writings, as his students in the English Department we always felt inspired to believe that there exists an urgent need for the kind of critical intelligence committed (in Leavis's words) to a 'human reality, an autonomy of the human spirit', which cares enough to ask society about the adequacy of its values and beliefs for a humane existence, and was convinced that standards of living, for example, could and should be defined in other than merely material or expedient terms. And this was after all, the spirit inherent in Enright's inaugural lecture, and which became obscured in the aggravations of the time.

In practice, Enright actively encouraged local writers and literary activities. At his suggestion and with his support, the Literary Society was founded in 1960, as well as its also still-surviving magazine, *Focus*. Arthur Yap, arguably Singapore's most adventurous and accomplished poet in English, acknowledges a debt when he says that 'Enright inculcated in us a feel for the English language which I have never lost'. Many of his students from the decade in which he was in Singapore are working in occupations

---

* For instance, in *The Mirror*, 7 July 1969, the Ministry of Culture publication, reports the Minister of Law and National Development, no less, as agreeing that 'the evolution of a common culture is not the monopoly of the government', and that 'There must be no factors to impede the free interplay of cultural forces.'

which have a potential for cultural influence: they form today, for instance, the core of the local academic staff of the Department of English Language and Literature, and are to be found not only in the education service, but also the media, and the middle and top echelons of the Singapore Civil Service. One of these, among the last of Enright's students, who was a promising poet, and is now Private Secretary to the President of Singapore, conveys something of Enright's propensity for outrageous, witty, but essentially serious utterance; his hilariously funny and often acid asides; the kind, tactful reticence in personal matters, and the discomfiting critical penetration of the not easily deceived, when he recalled that Enright 'was something of a clown with a heart, too intense to like, too complex to ignore, and altogether unforgettable.'

Dennis Enright
A Portrait

PAUL THEROUX

MOST people I meet tell me what an absolute sweetheart Dennis Enright is, yet he has always struck me as being rather tough, and capable of being fierce, as shy people often are. He is suspicious of success, of money, of power, of authority, of any sort of style, of anything that smacks of fraudulence—a bit of a Methodist, really, a convinced Leavisite: 'incorruptible', Leavis called him. And what is surprising is that I know he has been a tearaway, a softie, a rebel, a heavy smoker, a steady drinker, and a taker of opium.

His idea of fun is being in hot water. He is anything but a prig, but I think he regards hot water as the natural habitat of a moral person. Other people are better able to describe his upbringing— *The Terrible Shears* should be description enough—and I am convinced that this memoir of growing up poor in a council house in the Midlands is one of his masterpieces. His early life gave him a lasting sympathy for the underdog. As for his university days at Cambridge—the influence of good teaching and ingenious contemporaries shows in everything he has written. He has had one of the most diverse teaching careers of anyone I can think of: Egypt, Germany, Japan, Thailand, Singapore. What other writer has been so extensively occupied on a global scale? And Dennis was not a bird of passage. He took his work seriously, he learned local languages (he still speaks German and some Japanese I believe) and he made a point of understanding his students. I am somewhat sensitive about this, because in my own teaching career I know I was a slacker (this was in Nyasaland, Uganda, and Enright's Singapore) and unlike Dennis I put my writing first and my teaching second, and eventually Dennis's Singaporean successor—and protégé—called me into his office and told me tersely that my contract was not being renewed. That irritated me greatly, because I had planned to resign, and in a sense he had fired me before I could tell him to take that job and shove it. That was something Dennis was always saying, though with greater elegance.

He came very close to resigning when I was hired, in 1968. I was trying to think of an interesting alternative to Uganda, where I had had enough of chaos and old night. I didn't feel particularly vulnerable, which was surprising, because I had no money, my books weren't selling, my wife had just delivered a son, I had started to write what I knew would be a very long novel, I had resigned from Makerere University, and I was in the middle of Africa. I had a strong sense of being very lucky, and yet I could seldom convince anyone of that. To the casual observer, or reader of a job application, it must have looked as though I was fucked-up and far from home.

It was a situation Dennis understood perfectly, and he responded without hesitation. He offered me a job, starting almost immediately, at a good salary, as Lecturer in English at the University of Singapore. That was the first telegram. There was a second telegram, saying there had been a problem, that it was a serious snag and the last words were the ominous telegraphic formula, *letter follows*.

It was a sorrowful and apologetic letter, and it was also angry — on my behalf: it was Dennis at his combative best. Briefly, the authorities at the University of Singapore had seen various articles that I had written and they had become alarmed. At that time Indians in Kenya and Uganda were fighting for their survival, having been officially abused by the African governments, and I had written a number of pieces defending the Indians and mocking the racialism of the African position. My pieces had caused a certain amount of comment. It was construed in Singapore that I was a rabble-rouser (a small intimidated Indian minority also lived there), and the Vice Chancellor of the university ordered Dennis to withdraw the job offer that had been made to me. The fact that the Vice Chancellor was also a powerful cabinet minister gave this order considerable force.

But Dennis, being Dennis, stood his ground, and he said that he was morally obliged to be as good as his word. And if they went over his head and withdrew the job offer, then — he said — he would resign. It was not the first time he had offered his resignation on a point of principle, nor was it the last. The point was conceded to him, but it was a hollow victory. Okay, the authorities said, as they introduced a Chinese dimension—the terms of my contract.

That was the reason for the sorrow in Dennis's letter to me, because the terms were derisory. I was offered a one-year contract in Singapore at the lowest salary on the pay scale, 1,440 Straits dollars a month, which worked out to about £50 a week. In addition I had to give an undertaking that I would not write or publish anything, fiction or non-fiction, while I was in Singapore. There were no perks to the job, and Dennis explained that these laughable terms meant I wasn't wanted—it was merely a face-saving gesture. I was viewed as a threat, a hippy, an undesirable, and he suggested that I would probably be right to refuse.

I immediately cabled my acceptance. I had no other choice, and this seemed—in an interesting sense—like a leap in the dark. I still believed in my luck. I think that decision endeared me to Dennis, who had taken similar risks throughout his life. From the moment of my arrival he saw me as a friend and ally.

He struck me as informal and straightforward. He was an old-fashioned liberal. He found the Chinese humourless and puritanical, but he admired their dedication to work. He loathed politicians and party men, and he seemed to have an almost instinctive mistrust of any kind of authority. These were all admirable qualities, I felt. He also worked very hard, and it was clear that the students adored him. They called him 'Prof.'

'I don't want to be seen as a lovable old Mr Chips', he wrote in *Memoirs of a Mendicant Professor*, but it seemed to me that he was very near to being that. Not exactly lovable, but kind, attentive, and with the students' best interests at heart. He was in addition possessed of an almost missionary zeal in the teaching of English Literature. It was a moral discipline; it was culture; it was civilization. He believed in his subject, and he was passionate about it, in a way that made the other faculties—history, philo-sophy, maths, and so forth, seem rather half-hearted. He laughed at the thought that sociology might be considered a subject, a common prejudice of English academics at the time. Another prejudice, rife in the department but one that Dennis did not inspire, was against American literature. English dons often smiled and looked puzzled and said, *Is there such a thing?*

Dennis worked nine to five. 'Never absent, never late', he used to joke. But it was true. He encouraged the rest of the department to do likewise. I couldn't see the point of these long hours, frankly, but as a very junior lecturer how could I refuse? Some of the others kept their own hours, and Dennis had a way of reminding everyone that he disapproved. He would go from office to office, saying, 'Where's So-and-so? He's not in his office' — thus reminding us that when we weren't there he probably did the same, saying our names. I found this a nuisance — after all, I was trying to finish a novel. I kept this from Dennis, who believed that the job came first. He wrote poems, essays, and reviews at night and on the weekends; surely I could do the same? But it was hot and buggy at night, and on the weekends I preferred to go swimming with my wife and child.

Dennis did not swim. He hardly walked: he drove his beat-up blue car a few hundred yards from his house to the office. I seldom saw him get any exercise. He seemed to have few pleasures. Even in a restaurant, as the dishes were being served and eaten, Dennis would be sitting sideways, awkwardly in his chair, poking a cigarette into his stained and chewed holder. He was one of those fidgetty people who smoke while eating, and he used to claw at his hair and sigh, as though exasperated by the enjoyment of the other diners. He smoked cigarettes, he smoked a pipe, he had the odd cigar. His idea of relaxation was drinking beer in a Chinese shop — wobbly tables, smeared tiles, glazed chickens hanging in the front window — and talking about Dickens or D. H. Lawrence, or else gossiping. If he had a weakness it was for gossip, but it was not a serious weakness, and his own puritanism made his gossip somewhat steamy.

Singapore was a horribly dull place, and yet in the time I was there (my contract was renewed for an additional two years at the same low salary) extraordinary events occurred. The first took place not long after I arrived. Our External Examiner flew out from England. He was in his fifties and rather florid; he said he played squash with men half his age. He was a heavy eater, he drank thirstily, he panted and perspired. He was the subject of a certain amount of gossip and some gentle mockery.

The night before he left for England, we gave him a party at The Celestial Room — a Chinese restaurant. He danced and perspired and danced some more, and while dancing with a Chinese botanist he collapsed and died of a heart attack. And so, after a few days in Singapore, this man was being cremated and

Dennis was leading us in the singing of the dead External Examiner's favourite hymns. He went home in a ceramic pot. Dennis wrote a poem about this incident: 'Death in a Strange Land'. I used it in a novel, *Saint Jack*.

There was a brothel called Serene House across the road from the university, which became a hotel of sorts for American soldiers on Rest-and-Recreation Leave from Vietnam. A bus arrived full of soldiers who were greeted by prostitutes at the gates of Serene House, and then each soldier would team up with a girl for a week; after that, it was back to the war. Now and then these soldiers, bored with the cowboy films, the drinking, and the sex, would visit us, just to talk, or to use the library. Dennis was very hospitable to these young bewildered men. He wrote a poem about it ('R-and-R Centre'); and I used it in *Saint Jack*.

I had not gone to Singapore in search of 'material', nor had Dennis. And indeed, in spite of his ten years in Singapore, he wrote remarkably little about it; there was no novel (he had previously written novels set in Egypt and Bangkok). He wrote many essays and book reviews, but they might have been written anywhere. As I say, he kept indoors.

In this frustrating place, a prosperous little island where there was no intellectual or political debate—essentially a one-party state in the hands of one man, Harry Lee—Dennis placed his faith in the students. I had no such faith, I'm afraid. I imagined them all leaving eventually—going to Australia and the United States, fleeing this hothouse. Dennis had an old-fashioned belief in the idealism of the students and the inviolate nature of the university. Knowing this, and trusting him, the students worked very hard. And everyone more or less ignored the fact that the university was run by the government.

What made that period especially strange was the Cultural Revolution in China. The cant, the songs, the symbols, and even some of the violence had faint echoes in Singapore, as little groups of Chinese were stirred by events on the mainland. This terrified the Singapore government, and it accounted for a great deal of its paranoia and its mistrust of students. Any student who raised a voice in protest was suspected of being inspired by the Red Guards. Vietnam was hellishly nearby: another leaden echo.

Now and then, Dennis would say, 'I've just been offered a job in America', and he would name the university. He was not boasting. It happened quite frequently. The first few times I urged him to reconsider, and I described the delights of California or Texas. Dennis was not interested. He mocked the high salaries he was offered. He jeered at the happy American campus. What kind of mission would that be? I felt he was somewhat self-defeating. And on the occasion of every Honours' List there was a rumour that Dennis had refused a gong.

Yet he was becoming restless. He hated the changes that were being instituted, particularly the introduction of linguistics in the English Department, and the general meddling with the university. He said he was writing his memoirs. That had an intimation of departure in it, if not a sense of shutting-up shop entirely.

I had no idea what his plans were, and I had no plans. We were friends, but he knew my heart wasn't in my job. My best energies went into the novel I was writing. I could not understand why, after having published four novels, I still needed this job. And because of my pitiful salary my wife went out to work, teaching at Nanyang, the Chinese university. At times I felt I had failed miserably—taken a wrong turning, landed in the wrong place. I sat in the Staff Club with the other expatriates, Dennis among them, drinking beer and bitching as the rain came down. Was this any kind of life? I was 29 years old. Dennis was 50. I felt 50. The central character in my novel was 50.

My youth and my hopes were returned to me one day. I had spent all my money on an air-conditioned rental car, and driven with my family out of Singapore, up north, through Malaysia, to the cool uplands of the Cameron Highlands, and then to Penang. It was all wonderful—swimming, sunshine, pleasant food, and the easy manner of the Malays. It was a fling, but it was well-timed. When we returned to Singapore a telegram awaited me, saying that I had just sold the movie rights to my novel, *Girls At Play*. Because it was a telegram, and because I had been away, it had been read by a dozen people, and everyone at the Staff Club knew of it. Dennis wished me well—he was genuinely glad for me, but I think at that moment something between us ended. He knew I was going to be all right; he was not so sure about himself.

There are two versions of Dennis's resignation. In the first, he is in a meeting with a high university official, and they are disagreeing about something. Dennis becomes impatient, and uses the technique that has worked so many times before. 'If that's the way you want it, then I resign.' In the past the Chinese official compromised, lost most of his face and begged him to reconsider. This time he says, 'Put it in writing, Professor.'

The second version is the one I believe, because it is the best reason I have ever heard for someone giving up teaching.

'I'm leaving Singapore, because I've stopped learning anything from my students', Dennis said.

He went to London and the other expatriates in the department dispersed—to Australia, England, Malaysia. I became the Last of the Mohicans, and then I too left. It was not that I had given up teaching; I had given up any sort of salaried job. Off I went to England to live cheaply and be a full-time writer.

In the meantime, Dennis had begun working for a publisher. I saw him from time to time. I don't think he ever saw himself as a bowler-hatted T. S. Eliot figure on the publishing scene, but neither do I believe that he was prepared for the philistinism and money-grubbing that characterizes so many publishing efforts. He was appalled to see people he regarded as sensible, eagerly publishing crass American best-sellers in the hopes of having an English windfall.

'We just bought a book about weight-lifters', he said to me one day. 'Can you imagine? *Weight-lifters*?'

He occupied an office in a passage, through which, from time to time, secretaries and messengers squeezed, on their way from other offices. I asked him about the other directors. He said he didn't see much of them. The head of the firm, Norah Smallwood, had a great reputation. 'She threw her umbrella at me this morning', Dennis told me once. Then he said he had been promoted. 'I'm not getting a rise in salary, but they've offered me more Luncheon Vouchers.' Soon after, he was awarded the Queen's Gold Medal for Poetry.

I saw less and less of him. He kept writing; he's still at it. That's the main thing.

Scenes from Publishing Life

JEREMY LEWIS

BACK in the early 1970s, I was working as a literary agent, of shaming ineptitude. My authors were, on the whole, a fine and talented bunch, some of whom went on to become familiar names (one of the best is, I see, a fellow-contributor to this book): but an agent is, by definition, something of a fixer and a haggler, and since both these qualities are almost entirely absent from my make-up, I found it hard to give my writers the service they rightly expected. During my stint as an agent, I sold to Chatto & Windus a rather remarkable book, baldly entitled *Genius*, and written by a polymathic Oxford don who taught politics at Wadham. He specialized in the history of trade unionism and of Methodism, but had had the temerity to stray into areas not formally his own. A study of the Romantic cult of genius, it drew heavily on German writers and philosophers, such as E. T. A. Hoffmann, Hegel, and Schiller.

Chatto, with its long and distinguished list of literary critics— F. R. and Q. D. Leavis, Raymond Williams, William Empson, Richard Hoggart, Basil Willey, L. C. Knights, Muriel Bradbrook, and D. J. Enright among them—had seemed a fairly obvious publisher for such a book, but it was a firm of which I then knew very little. Despite the distinction of its list and the presence on its letterhead (and that of the Hogarth Press) of such names as Leonard Woolf and, until recently, C. Day Lewis, literary agents were not as eager as they might have been to deal with the firm, on the grounds that Chatto was considered a trifle dusty and old-fashioned when it came to the presentation and promotion of their wares, and somewhat tight-fisted in the matter of advances to their authors; while negotiating terms could all too easily involve one in doing battle with the formidable Mrs Norah Smallwood, one of the two managing directors, and a figure calculated to bring beads of sweat to the brow of the most hard-boiled veteran.

Very much to my relief there had been no sign of Mrs Smallwood when it came to drawing up a contract for *Genius*—perhaps I had excelled myself and asked for less than they were prepared to offer, or even for nothing at all?—and with that out of the way, I could sit back and enjoy the wholesome glow that comes from doing good. As for the book itself, it was in the capable hands of D. J. Enright, to whom I had first sent it. A Chatto author since 1960, he had returned to Britain in 1970, and in 1974 joined the Chatto board, succeeding Day Lewis in charge of the poetry list and involving himself in a certain amount of general and fiction publishing. And since he had a particular interest in German literature, and was as pleasingly cosmopolitan in his reading as in his places of residence, he was the ideal editor for this book.

Being so obviously unsuited to the life I was leading, I filled in the long hours of office life carousing in the Lamb in Lamb's Conduit Street, and then, after the last clerks had been sent stumbling on their way and the doors locked behind us, sitting gloomily at my desk, snoozing fitfully and writing letters to publishers begging to be allowed back into the trade I had so ungratefully spurned for the life of a literary agent. As I had by now sold Chatto a couple of books (or ideas for books), I thought, in a sudden spasm of self-aggrandisement, that I would write to Mrs Smallwood and ask her if she would like to offer me a job. A day or two later her secretary rang to say that, alas, there was nothing on offer, but that Mrs Smallwood would be prepared to see me on a particular afternoon at such-and-such a time. I dreaded my meeting with this legendary figure who would, I felt sure, send me away with my tail between my legs: perhaps I could sweeten the pill by meeting first Dennis Enright, who sounded—on the phone at least—the most unalarming of men, and not someone likely to bite me on the leg in the course of my professional duties? We agreed that I would call to see him, and that he would then shunt me down the corridor for my appointment with his Leader.

On the appointed afternoon I turned up, for the first time, at the old Chatto offices in William IV Street, opposite the Post Office at the bottom of St Martin's Lane. After pushing my way through a pair of blue swing doors, I found myself in a bare and gloomy corridor. A broad staircase of incongruous grandeur swept upwards into darkness, baroque barley-sugar banister rails blending oddly with the dark-blue lino on the treads; ahead, behind a sliding-glass panel, a figure with the head of a heavy-smoking and highly distinguished Roman emperor, sat at the controls of an elderly, upright switchboard, a cigarette smoking from one hand while with the other he plunged a plug into a hole in the switchboard (so connecting the caller and the called), or, with a bold, imperious gesture, yanked another from its resting-place (more often than not, as I was later to learn, cutting off the parties in mid-sentence). Tentatively moving the glass panel aside, I asked George—for such was his name—where and how I could find Professor Enright; he gave a nimble display on the plugs, announced my arrival, and suggested I took the lift to the second floor, where the Professor would await me.

As it turned out, I would have been better advised to set off up the baronial staircase, since the lift was of that unrestful pre-war variety that involved holding open with one's elbows two tightly sprung wooden doors while struggling to pull aside a black metal grille, like part of an old-fashioned camera, that lunged hungrily at one's head and shoulders and nipped the ankles of the unwary. After a good deal of opening and closing of doors, and wrestling with the metal grille, we began to move, very slowly, in the direction of the second floor. Once there the lift stopped with a sudden jerk, throwing me off balance; after which I had once more to do battle with the grille, holding it firmly in place with my foot while struggling to push open another pair of equally well-sprung wooden doors. (Years later, when I came to work at Chatto, I disdained the services of this boisterous lift. Mrs Smallwood, on the other hand—frail, arthritic, carrying a walking stick—made regular use of it; but it may well be that she had, early on in her long career, quelled it with a glance.)

I stumbled, dishevelled, on to a darkened landing, the walls of which—like those of a prep school or a lunatic asylum—were painted in dark blue gloss up to waist level, and pale blue above; on the floor was the same blue lino I had noticed in the corridor below and on the stairs. Peering through the gloom, I saw before me a ruefully smiling figure with a wide, expressive mouth, a bush of grey hair that shot away from his head like a coil of smoke in a high wind, and pale, rather rubbery features that combined—in the most engaging way—the lugubrious and the comical, the sardonic and the benign. He was clad—almost certainly—in a fawn or green shirt with a green or fawn tie; fawn trousers; shoes with tractor soles; and a bottle-green corduroy (or, perhaps, a fawn cotton) jacket. I like to think he had a pipe in his mouth; be that as it may, he shook me by the hand in a resigned and doleful way, and—like a kindly jailer—beckoned me to follow him past an array of pigeon-holes and down a maze of corridors, all painted in the same institutional shades. We passed a door with the words 'Norah Smallwood' painted on it, on a small wooden plaque; and as we did so—or so I like to think—Dennis raised his eyes to heaven with a woeful look, or pressed his fingers to his lips, so that we stole past the dragon's lair on the tips of our toes.

After another imposing-looking door with 'Ian Parsons' emblazoned on it—'IMP', as he was known, was then joint managing director—we turned left, right, and left again before coming to Dennis's lair: a small, sunny room with a greenhouse door, khaki-coloured bookshelves on two walls, post-war Utility furniture, and the same blue lino on the floor. On Dennis's table was a black upright typewriter, several typescripts, a set of proofs, an ashtray, a reading-lamp and an elderly bakelite telephone with a brown twisted cord running away from it. Taking a look out of the window, I realized that the Chatto offices were built around a well, on the other side of which other members of the firm could be spotted making coffee or tugging at filing cabinets or filing their nails or trading office gossip in conspiratorial, outraged tones, or gazing blankly back across the well in a day-dream. Above us, to the right, the illuminated globe on top of the London Coliseum spun slowly round and round, while through the open window came the sudden screech of a soprano practising her scales, like a knife upon a plate. This had, I learned, been C. Day Lewis's office before Dennis's arrival; much later, as part of a general falling-off, I was to spend some years in it myself—Dennis had moved to a room on the floor above—editing typescripts, writing blurbs, studying the small print in contracts, correcting proofs, coming back far too late from over-convivial lunches, and listening, with a kind of frozen terror, to Mrs Smallwood's voice advancing down the corridor, and the tap of her stick on the lino.

Not that Dennis had, it seemed, any airs or affectations about himself and his work as a writer, or publisher. He combined modesty, self-deprecation, and a humorously mocking and affectionate attitude towards those with whom he had to deal, with a strong if world-weary sense of what was right and good;

and a firm sense of his own worth, with sympathy and understanding for the defeated and the average and the unliterary, and
a deep dislike of the cynicism and the affectations of superiority
or omniscience that come all too naturally to the well-educated
and the articulate. As he told me about life at Chatto, and what
he did there—his voice a throwaway mutter, interspersed with
laughter and the sudden pulling of faces—he busied himself
cleaning and filling and tamping his pipe; as is often the case with
professional pipe-smokers, these preparatory rituals seem to take
up a good deal more time than the actual smoking.

   After half an hour or so of chatting peaceably, we were inter-
rupted by a blast from the telephone. Dennis gave the rude
intruder an admonishing sideways glance from under momentarily
darkened brows, and then with a sigh and a shrug, picked up
the receiver. A loud, imperious female voice rang round the room.
At the first syllable, Dennis sat upright to attention in his chair,
as though he had been unexpectedly plugged into the mains; and
as the voice spoke on, he held the receiver out at arm's length,
every now and then bringing it back to his mouth when his views
were sought. The voice eventually revealed that its owner was
ready to receive Mr Lewis, and would Dennis kindly show him
the way? Dennis rose wearily from behind his desk, and we
retraced our steps back along the labyrinthine corridors. On the
threshold of Mrs Smallwood's office we paused, and he placed
an avuncular hand on my shoulder, as though I were a young
officer about to go over the top, before knocking and ushering
me in. My last glimpse of him was standing rigidly to attention
in the doorway, like a self-mocking military man; and then,
'Thank you, Dennis', called the cool, commanding voice from
within, and he disappeared back into the darkness.

   Mrs Smallwood didn't offer me a job on that occasion, but some
years later I would be working for her, alongside Dennis.

In the meantime I'd seen something of him in Oxford, where
I had a brief spell as an editor for the Oxford University Press,
whose trade publishing had been moved in the autumn of 1976
from Ely House to join the Clarendon Press. Dennis visited us
in November 1977 with Ernst de Chickera, a former colleague
from Singapore who had gone on to teach at La Trobe University
in Australia, and co-editor with Dennis of a successful textbook

published by the Press. Several editors eagerly forsook their desks to take them to lunch in OUP's formal dining-rooms in Walton Street. The dining-rooms combined, in the most endearing way, the Senior Common Room with the works canteen, chandeliers with soggy chips, engravings of college life and portraits of former Secretaries to the Delegates with spotted dick and custard with skin on top. The drinks cupboard was generously stocked; the jocular waitresses seemed to like nothing better than the sound of corks being pulled; boxes of cigars lay open on the sideboard crying out to be puffed with the brandy, or gathered up in fistfuls to line the inner pockets of one's jacket. Not surprisingly this turned out to be an unusually convivial lunch, breaking up at half-past four, as the cleaning women hoovered round our legs, and reassembling in the Randolph late in the afternoon, before Dennis and Ernst—nobly bearing between them the satchel full of manuscripts that weighed down our poetry editor—took the last train back to London.

Dennis later decided to move his own poems from Chatto to Oxford (not unreasonably, he found being a 'house' editor, responsible for publishing his own work, an invidious business). His *A Faust Book* was just published and the first of his Oxford anthologies (*of Contemporary Verse*) commissioned before I left. OUP has published nearly a book a year by him since: poems, essays, anthologies—but not, I think, ever a second volume of the educational textbook . . .

In the months before Hugo Brunner and I joined (in Hugo's case, rejoined) Chatto from OUP, I called several times at William IV Street to meet my future colleagues. By now Dennis was, at the very least, a familiar face; and on one of these preliminary trips I met his closest friend there, Leslie Booth. Advancing into the stygian quarters that lay on the ground-floor beyond George's reception area and the grandiose staircase sweeping up into the darkness, I came upon a region of cardboard and string and jiffy bags, of post-office scales and wooden-handled knives and pots of glue: the place in which mail was sorted and despatched, and unsolicited typescripts or advance copies of new books sent winging on their way. In this subterranean zone three men were sitting on brown paper parcels of the Collected Works of Sigmund Freud (I like to think that all three had pipes in their mouths, but this may have been too much to hope for): Dennis; the then

editorial director, a tall, fine-looking man with the features of
Sherlock Holmes; and a humorous-looking individual clad in a
brown cotton overgarment of the kind worn by old-fashioned
ironmongers or grocers, whose long, narrow face, bushy eyebrows,
and mutton-chop whiskers gave him the look of a successful mid-
Victorian poacher. He was introduced to me as Les Booth, the
office packer. As soon as I joined the firm I found Les a kindred
spirit, and joined him and Dennis for their weekly lunchtime
session in the Welsh Harp or the Marquis of Granby: a tradition
which, eleven years later, is maintained, though Les no longer
makes it after moving to the far end of the Metropolitan Line.
A man of infinite wisdom, Les was—as is so often the case—
very much shrewder and better-informed about office politics than
many of my directorial colleagues. In this he was helped no end
by George's overhearing snatches of Mrs Smallwood's telephone
conversations with members of the Top Board which, in those
pre-Random House days, ran the affairs of the Chatto, Bodley
Head, and Cape group (caught in mid-stream, George would
press a raised forefinger to his lips, never losing for a moment
his frown of concentration). He would then pass the news on to
Les, who would pass it on to me, and we would all be that much
better informed. Only in his alleged defiance of Mrs Smallwood
was Les, perhaps, a shade unreliable: over drinks in the Marquis
he would tell us—striking the table with his hand—how he had,
in effect, driven Mrs Smallwood from the packing-room ('You
stick to editing those books, and leave the parcels to me') but
somehow it never quite rang true.

Dennis's friendship with Les caused a certain raising of eyebrows
in a firm in which the Bloomsbury traditions of leftish principles
combined with old-fashioned snobbery still prevailed. Unlike his
fellow-directors, Dennis came from a working-class background;
he was also a natural democrat, choosing his friends—as he chose
his books—because he liked and respected them, rather than
because they came from a particular class, or had been educated
to a particular level, or were (or were not) fellow-writers or
academics. Literary publishing is, almost by definition, a snobbish
trade, since publishers hunger after, and depend upon, the
famous and the well-connected, and intellectual snobbery and
social snobbery are compatible more often than one might think;
within a rather snobbish and surprisingly stratified firm like

Chatto, Dennis acted—more than anyone else—as a kind of social lubricant, accessible and kindly (to their faces, if not always when letting off steam over a pint in the pub) to the highest and the lowest; and in a firm in which members of staff were sometimes treated more sharply than is customary (I sometimes felt that the walls of William IV Street were, like those of a seaside hotel, briney with secretarial tears) he was often there to comfort and assuage and, more importantly, to make the victims see their travails in some kind of perspective.

Heaven forbid that I should give the impression that Dennis's role at Chatto was simply that of an unusually well-read district nurse or human fire-extinguisher: but the ability to see things in perspective was one of Dennis's great qualities—and limitations— as a publishing editor and adviser. Publishing—and literary publishing in particular—is a curious combination of art and commerce, of the long and the short term, of (for the most part) the ephemeral and (very occasionally) the lasting; and the ideal publisher needs to combine the abilities of the man of letters, the entrepreneur, the impresario, and the accountant. Even the most rarefied of firms needs to publish a certain number of books per annum—including, ideally, a dependable line in reference books or children's books or professional books to pay for the more speculative titles—if only to cover the rates and the electric light and the usually rather modest salaries of those who work there, let alone the costs of paper and printing, the royalties owing to authors and, with luck, a small profit to keep the venture afloat for another year. In even the most literary of firms the great majority of these titles will, inevitably, be evanescent and, by the highest standards, second- or third-rate; but the good publisher must—and not entirely cynically—persuade himself and others, if for a season only, that a particular novel or biography or travel book is 'the best thing of its kind I've read for years' or a 'masterpiece', and that the forthcoming seasonal list is (once again) 'the best I've ever known'. This suspension of disbelief— or, rather, this momentarily quite genuine readiness to make, and believe, somewhat exaggerated claims—is essential to the working of the literary business and to the well-being of those who depend upon it, and is happily indulged in by reviewers, literary editors, literary agents, booksellers, dwellers in Hampstead, and, it goes without saying, those authors who benefit from it in terms of sales and reputation (and sometimes both) as well as by publishers; and without it the world would, no doubt, be a duller place. Caught up in the turmoil of claim and counter-claim, it's sometimes hard to take the long-term view, or to remember — when confronted with ecstatic claims for some tedious modern novel — that, from the great age of the Victorian novel, only a handful of names survive.

Dennis was far too sceptical, far too aware of the long term, and far too committed to the highest of standards to have made a publisher, as opposed to a cautionary and meticulous editor: left to his own devices he would, perhaps, have published two or three books a year, which may well have made sense *sub specie aeternitatis* (if erring, perhaps, on the side of excess) but would never have paid the bills or earned his firm a reputation for publishing new talent or taking a risk with exciting young authors. (It has to be said, though, that much of the most interesting and adventurous publishing of this century has, in fact, been undertaken by what were, in the very best sense, 'amateur' or 'part-time' publishers — writers like Alan Ross and the Woolfs and John Lehmann who, untroubled by enormous overheads or large staffs waiting to be paid, ran what were, in effect, one-man bands, and were in the enviable position of publishing only those few books they really believed in or wanted to take on.) Nor did Dennis have the avarice or the proprietorial urge so essential to the successful publisher: he seemed loath to mix friendship and business in the sense of inveigling fellow-authors on to the list; and whereas the human dynamo feels — for an hour or two at least — a sense of deep outrage if a particular author chooses another firm instead of his own, Dennis seemed perfectly happy so long as *someone* was going to publish that writer's book (assuming he thought it any good) and indifferent if he thought little of it anyway. (He remains unrepentant about having turned down — and so lost to Chatto — one of our most successful 'literary' novelists.)

And yet, in an ideal world, all self-respecting literary publishers would have a Dennis to hand, with his knowledge, his wide reading, his high standards, his scepticism, his eye for the excellent (and the meretricious), his mumbled mockery of the exaggerated claims and the evanescent enthusiasms that are an equally necessary and inevitable part of the publishing process.

Years before when I worked, very enjoyably, for André Deutsch, it seemed to me Nicolas Bentley had played a similarly therapeutic and salutary role, bringing things down to earth, letting a breath of the outside world filter into what can all-too-easily become claustrophobic, self-regarding, and self-indulgent. After talking to him, or to Dennis, one saw things in their proper place.

It would be quite wrong, though, to suggest that Dennis failed to take his work or his responsibilities with due seriousness during his years at Chatto. He asked, and expected, high standards from those authors with whom he worked, and grumbles to this day about an eminent author whose new 'book' consisted of pages torn from assorted magazines and stuffed into an envelope. His reports were miraculously succinct, witty, and acute; he was that rare and invaluable asset, an exemplary writer of blurbs; time and again Norah Smallwood would, when in need of expert support, summon 'Professor Enright' to discuss the finer points of an author's work or give substance to an argument; at sales conferences—where he was, understandably, the most popular of all the editors with the sales force, and not only on account of the hip-flask of whisky with which he reinforced the acidulous office wine during the lunch break—he took endless trouble to explain his books, never talking down to the reps in any way; to those works—like Terence Kilmartin's revision of the Scott Moncrieff Proust—on which he was deeply engaged he not only brought a level of scholarship and editorial exactitude that must have been rare, if not unique, in British publishing, but wisely and bravely beat off any efforts to put it on the market before it was ready ('But, Dennis, we need the turnover . . .'—the publisher's permanent cry).

Norah Smallwood may have been—often was—as ferocious and as difficult to work for as people always said she was: but she had a shrewd eye for quality and for the genuine article, and if she was puzzled by Dennis's preference for several pints washed down with whisky and water in the Marquis to grander literary occasions, she greatly valued his judgement, his wisdom, and his knowledge. Her affection and her regard were amply repaid: Dennis may, in turn, have disapproved her ferocity and her waspishness to those who worked for her—and mocked her weakness for titled grandees—but he admired, rightly, her courage, her clarity of mind, her humour, her taste, and her ruthless ability to cut through waffle and obfuscation to reach the heart of the matter; and he felt for her, as most of us did in civilian life at least, a liking and a respect of the kind that one could never feel for someone wholly tyrannical and harsh. One of Dennis's trickier jobs at Chatto was explaining the steamier passages from modern novels to Mrs Smallwood: asked, on one occasion, to explain over the internal telephone an intimate sexual practice of a kind unfamiliar, perhaps, in Bloomsbury (and, come to that, in a good many other places as well), he began, with much clearing of the throat, to edge his way towards elucidation via the Latin words for, in the first instance, 'tongue' — the trickier part came first, in fact — only to have that cool, incisive voice cut clean across his mumbled explanation with 'I see, Dennis. One of those filthy words', followed by the crash of the receiver being replaced on its stand.

Of Dennis's work as a poetry publisher I am ill-equipped to speak. He added new authors to the Phoenix Living Poets inherited from Ian Parsons and C. Day Lewis (John Hartley Williams, and his fellow poet–publisher James Michie marked the end of the line); no doubt he bestowed upon Rodney Pybus and P. J. Kavanagh and Robert Conquest the same care and the same shrewd advice that he offered to A. S. Byatt or Richard Hoggart or (a particular discovery of his) the novelist Keith Colquhoun. His last couple of years in the office (by then four days a week) were dominated by the revised translation of Proust, a huge task that fascinated him, though the pressure to publish as soon as possible must have strained his perfectionism and good-humoured tact to bursting-point.

Much of even the best publisher's work is, by its very nature, ephemeral, and the recapitulation of old triumphs and once-compelling dramas tend, to those not directly involved, to have more than a touch of the yellowing press-clipping or the club bore's interminable drone. Dennis was not the kind of publisher who boasted in the Garrick of paperback rights sold for enormous sums of money, or giant advances, or forthcoming serialization in the *Sunday Times*; his work as an editor survives in the publisher's ultimate and only *raison d'être*, on the pages of the authors with whom he worked. For my part — having an incurably trivial mind — my memories of Dennis at Chatto are of his advancing down a corridor, his hair on end and his face illuminated with a lopsided grin, to impart in a sardonic mutter the full details of some new act of folly on the part of a colleague or an author; or—though this took place after he had, to the sorrow of us all, or almost all of us, left the firm in 1982—of his sampling and re-sampling with Les the various bottles of home-made wine brewed up by our author, Mollie Harris, and making such inroads on the rose-hip, the parsley, and the nettle that the bottles had to be topped up with water before they could be enjoyed by the reps at the forthcoming sales conference; or of his playing truant from a more formal affair in the office in order to join Les and me in pre-Christmas drinks in the Welsh Harp, and leading a hurried exit from the back door after I had spotted Mrs Smallwood and a fellow-director inching their way purposefully through the crowd towards us to retrieve their errant colleague. But perhaps it would be best to end with something from Dennis himself, which not only conveys the flavour of the man, but gives a pleasing insight into the everyday life of a publisher's editor. Dennis had commissioned a selection of writings by the French humorist, Alphonse Allais, edited and translated by Miles Kington; and a gentleman from Monks Risborough who had bought a copy had written a comical–facetious letter complaining (with some justice) that it was 'not only the worst example of typesetting I can remember seeing from a reputable publisher', but that the offending volume—which, typesetting apart, he had found highly entertaining—had spontaneously combusted in the night, ruining in the process his first edition of *Orlando* and a book by Stanley Morison belonging to Bucks County Library. Dennis replied (on 1 December 1976):

Your letter apropos of Alphonse Allais has been passed to me since it was I who conceived the idea of the book. (However, I did not set it or produce it myself, though I am typing this letter myself.)

We had trouble with the book from the beginning. Not with M. Allais, who is dead, nor even with Miles Kington, though he is alive. For instance, the laminators reported that the jackets refused to accept lamination: this was later disproved. The printer sent the sheets to the wrong binder, where they lay unnoticed for some considerable time. Eventually the sheets were forwarded to the right binders, but alas the right binders' binding machine had by now gone wrong. Later, advance copies of the book, printed, bound and laminated against great odds, were put on the wrong train, or possibly the wrong part of the right train, and consigned to a siding.

To these accidents must now be added the ills experienced by your good self. (I say 'good' because purchasers of books are rare and good beings.) I am deeply grieved. We fear there is nothing we can do about your ex-mint *Orlando*, or the Bucks County Library copy of Stanley Morison's book. (Could it be that the germs of this spontaneous combustion were caught in that Library? Public libraries are not the most sanitary of places.) We can only offer you, with our compliments, a mint copy of the first edition of a recently published book by the author of *Orlando*. In view of its title* we must hope there will be no further outbreaks of fire on your bookshelves.

Yours sincerely,
D. J. Enright

* *Freshwater*, by Virginia Woolf.

It Is Too Easy for the Literary Man To Forget . . .
D. J. Enright as book reviewer

DERWENT MAY

IN the late 1970s, when I was literary editor of *The Listener* and Dennis Enright was working at Chatto & Windus, we would meet for lunch almost every Wednesday at the Marquis of Granby, a pub in Cambridge Circus. Sometimes he had had a trying morning in the office, and once, I remember, he came in looking particularly harassed.

'What'll you have, Dennis?'

'Half a pint of hemlock, dear boy. Don't make it a pint—it'll only be wasted.'

It can be imagined that those meetings were one of the pleasures of my week. And often he would bring a brown-paper envelope with him, which he would slip to me surreptitiously, as though it contained pornographic pictures or some illegal pay-off. That was the book review I was waiting for. I would read it when I got back to *The Listener*, and time and again would find an opening paragraph as arresting as the gambits I had got used to in the pub.

Here, for instance, is the beginning of his review of *Only One Year*, the memoirs of Svetlana Alliluyeva, Stalin's daughter, after her flight to the West: 'At times you think you are listening to the voice of Mother Russia. At times to the voice of a retired viceroy dictating his memoirs. At times to the voice of a stage Russian in a provincial theatre. At times to the Voice of America' (30 Oct. 1969). With beginnings like that, who needs conclusions?

During the twenty or so years that I was editing the book pages of *The Listener*, from 1965 to 1986, Enright wrote, according to my count, 165 reviews for me. Practically all of them were the kind of review that literary editors dream of: gripping the attention from the start, briskly developing a compelling argument, weaving in witty asides without for a moment letting go of the thread, and ending as memorably as they had begun.

Here are just a couple of the shrewd and comic thrusts to be found everywhere in them. David Storey's novel *A Prodigal Child* is about a working-class boy helped in his education by a rich married woman. But Enright thought that 'a soundproof curtain surrounds the characters' emotions, and nothing comes through but cryptic, disembodied statements'. He concluded: 'Reticence has its charms, especially nowadays, and in its peculiar way *A Prodigal Child* is memorable. It would be more memorable if only one knew what one was remembering' (1 July 1982).

And I have always relished his spirited remark about the durability of literature, in his review of *Animals of Silence*, a book by a critic, Idris Parry, who in Enright's view made use of literary works just to provide material for his own 'potted profundity': 'All the same, a truly created work isn't made of butter, and can stand a lot of odd handling' (21 Sept. 1972).

But reading through these reviews again, it is not just good remarks that have delighted me. Consistently, over these twenty years, Enright gave voice to a very clear and sympathetic view of literature and its relation to life; and the reviews virtually add up to a literary credo. At times he would attack a critic for failing to see that poetry and fiction have a way of their own, and cannot be taken too literally. Reviewing a book on Goethe by Ronald Gray, for example, he writes:

On the Roman elegies Mr Gray is a shade prissy. He complains of the Third Elegy that 'no distinction is drawn between the love of Hero and Leander and the brutal taking of a princess by Mars'. But the outcome of Mars's happy fault was Romulus and Remus and, as Goethe indicates, the founding of Rome, all very apposite to the poem. If one is to apply modern morals to mythological allusions then one will soon be a very discontented reader! (3 Aug. 1963)

Far more often, however, Enright would himself take to task a poet or a novelist for losing grip of their own sense of reality. He came back more than once to the case of Ezra Pound, and in a long piece on 25 June 1970, he tries to define some of Pound's strengths and weaknesses. He starts with a typical glancing blow at a weakness of the biographer, Noel Stock, whose book *The Life of Ezra Pound* he is reviewing: 'on some personal matters more momentous than lemonade-drinking he is almost wincingly reticent.' But then he goes on to Pound himself. His main point in this review is that

despite T. S. Eliot's claim that Pound was the inventor of Chinese poetry for our time, I think it was a disaster when in 1913 Pound acquired the literary remains of Ernest Fenollosa [those notebooks contained Fenollosa's translations of and thoughts on Chinese poetry] . . . I believe that Pound's unguided and undisciplined transactions with Eastern literature led swiftly to a widening of the gap between word and thing, between the daughters of earth and the sons of heaven.

(It will be remembered that one of Enright's own volumes of poetry is called *Daughters of Earth*.) That, Enright says, is what led Pound in due course to his admiration for Mussolini and for Italian Fascism. And Enright finds a quotation from Pound himself to support his point: 'Isn't this a case of the sickness Pound had described in *How to Read*?—"when the application of word to thing goes rotten, i.e. becomes slushy and inexact, or excessive or bloated, the whole machinery of social and of individual thought and order goes to pot." ' But, this diagnosis made, Enright cannot end without coming back to his respect for Pound, and chooses his words with customary care: 'So much remains that is admirable and inspiring: the man's inexhaustible energy, his courage and fortitude, and of course his perceptiveness in many though not all literary matters. As for the other side of it, he paid the price . . .'.

Another writer whose merits and faults Enright has pondered on a great deal over the years is Lawrence Durrell. He wrote a famous attack on *The Alexandria Quartet* in the *International Literary Annual* (1961). In *The Listener* on 26 September 1968, he reviewed a book, *Lawrence Durrell*, by G. S. Fraser. He has some lightly ironical sport with this book. Fraser's description of Durrell, he says 'would be positively mouth-watering if one could read it as an account of some great author whose works one had yet to meet'. Unfortunately, readers 'may lose faith in Mr Fraser's proselytising powers quite early, when they run into a technical analysis of a piece of flagrantly mannered prose from *The Black Book*. We are reminded that as clever things can be said of bad art as good, and that without judgment the most professional of analysts is but a tinkling cymbal.'

His own judgement is that the plots of Durrell's novel are ludicrous, and that

> Durrell's genuine talents are for poetry and for the invention of grotesques, caricatures whose aim is not to satirise but to entertain. The books which have brought him fame are an unholy mixture and misuse of those talents. . . . *The Alexandria Quartet* is a fashionable fantasy, drenched in Chanel and furnished with every mod.-psych. convenience, and its public intrigues are as dream-like as its private ones.

The bases of his judgement come out clearly again in what he says of the book by Durrell which he most admires, his book about Cyprus, *Bitter Lemons*. '*Bitter Lemons* is more truly interesting because here reality breaks in, against Durrell, against the grain of his dreaming, with its real anger and its real pain, and Durrell has to contend with what other men have made, and not merely with the ductile and docile figures of his own fantasy.'

Enright came back to Durrell six years later with a review of a new novel by him, *Monsieur* (17 Oct. 1974). He began: 'This could not be by anyone other than Lawrence Durrell. . . . Who else would kick off with a night train southbound from Paris, its bluish lights strung out "like some super-glow-worm", the mistral purring outside like a cat, towards a mysterious suicide and an enigmatic madness?' But he found a genuine strength in this new novel—and turned the tables on the Durrell fans: 'Yet at the heart of this novel there is a sober and a solid piece of construction. It may for this reason disappoint Durrell's large body of prior admirers: perhaps, some of us may feel, it is time they were disappointed.' Enright has always approached a new book with a willingness to reconsider any previous opinion he had of the author.

The same principles of judgement can be discerned behind his review of a volume of John Ashbery's poems, *Self-Portrait in a Convex Mirror*, on 18 August 1977. Ashbery's poems are like 'humming and ha'ing raised to the highest point', he says, 'commentaries on poems Ashbery might have written if he were not writing commentaries on them.' As usual, Enright wants the poet to reach out beyond himself to something perceived and retained for the world's benefit. 'What a good poet Ashbery would be, if he took to writing poetry!'

Behind this insistence on the artist's duty to hold tight to a sense of reality, and not to be deflected from it by his self-indulgent broodings and fantasies, we can sense a further, and I think we may say a deeper strain in Enright's personality. This is a respect and tenderness for human beings at large — including, as can be seen, the perverse poets and novelists and critics themselves, whom he mocks and teases and calls back to their proper tasks, but to whom he is hardly ever cruel.

This comes out particularly in some of his reviews of auto-biographies and biographies. He returned often in these years to his dislike of books that exploited the lives of real people for prurient or sensational purposes. His opening paragraph in a review of *Great Tom*, a book about T. S. Eliot by T. S. Matthews, is as sharp-tongued as anything he ever wrote for *The Listener* (15 Aug. 1974):

The embarrassment felt in reviewing this book is analogous to that incurred in attacking pornography: one is likely to perpetuate or even aggravate the offence. In the present case, however, the reviewer can take courage from the near-certitude that the book's stark, staring silliness robs it of any power to hurt, damage or mislead.

And he goes on to judge Matthews severely for his crude invasions of Eliot's private life and his eager, insensitive criticisms of the poet:

His procedure resembles that of some Committee on Unacceptable Activities, and his investigation is to provide us with a rich assortment of Dreadful Warnings. . . . The voice of the District Attorney grates relentlessly on, mixing prurience ('Did Russell seduce Vivienne?') with petulance (the accused failed to spell a Spanish name correctly) and with farce ('Why did he never develop a stomach ulcer?').

Enright concludes the review: 'A man's work belongs to others, and fair enough, they make of it what they can or will. He ought to be able to call his life his own.'

Enright is almost as harsh in his review of the 'biographical speculations' of the late respected Richard Ellmann in his book *Golden Codgers* (4 Oct. 1977). Biographers, Enright says,

partake of the nature of historians, their profession calls for chastity, and they should seek as little as possible to weigh the imponderables. . . . When biographers behave like novelists, conjectures slide smoothly into

probabilities, and emerge a little later as established facts. . . . Professor
Ellmann comes dangerously close to muck-raking, which we hesitate to
reject on rational grounds, such is our high-minded concern for the truth,
but can generally detect by the smell it gives off.

When he reviewed Michel Leiris's autobiography, *Manhood*, on
7 March 1968, it was again the indifference to other human beings
and their claims that he found most disagreeable in the book. He
recognized, of course, that the book was a confessional, a study
in self-absorption and masochism, but he could not help insisting
that 'the humans adumbrated here have no more personal
presence or independent existence than do the scissors with
which Leiris lacerated himself. . . . It is too easy for the literary
man to forget that his path is set among human beings, not
among myths.'

In fact, along with his wit, it is Enright's warmth that makes
him in the end such an endearing critic. We feel it when he sums
up Leiris's book: this 'short self-exposure manages to seem long,
obsessive, intellectually over-heated and emotionally cold—
especially cold.' And this warmth, and love of warmth, is
sometimes displayed quite simply and clearly in his writing.
Reviewing Roger Shattuck's book, *The Forbidden Experiment*, about
the Wild Boy of Aveyron (14 Aug. 1980), he records how this
strange little boy of the woods was handed over by his scientist-
protector, Dr Itard, to the care of a Mme Guérin. Enright goes
fully and delicately into the questions about human nature raised
by the behaviour of this boy, who seemed to have been reared
in his infancy like an animal. But he ends: 'Perhaps the one who
gained most from this experiment was Mme Guérin, and perhaps
it was she who proved the most about human nature, the loving
kindness of which it is sometimes capable.'

Enright also wrote excellent reviews for *The Listener* about other
subjects than literature: about Vietnam and Singapore, about
opium and comic seaside postcards, about vampires (which
mythological creatures, he thinks, symbolize the attentions of a
particularly predatory kind of woman). During this period he also
wrote an amusing poem, 'Memoirs of a Book Reviewer' about
the strange phantasmagoria to be found in the brain of a reviewer
as he goes hectically from one book to the next, trying to live and
follow the news meanwhile. It ends:

Much drinking of *vin de pays* went on. I can
Remember a hangover. And lots of sex
In a lost world at the bottom of the Antarctic
Discovered by E. Pound, an American balloonist
And I lost my memory for several days, but
Found it at the bottom of a cheque. In a
Spare hour I tried to write a poem on life and
Death in a Vietnamese hamlet called SW18
Ravaged by peace and brutal schoolchildren
W. Pater came about the cooker
At some stage an exhaustive life of E. Pound
Appeared. A peasant named Confucius was raped
By the brutal intelligentsia. A large man came
About the rates, a book came about the rapes, a
Large book came about Shakespeare from Voltaire
To Ungaretti. An index slipped, trouble with
An appendix, my teeth hurt. At one point (I am
Almost sure) a book reviewer died at his desk
Whose name will be found at the bottom

(CP, 108–9)

Luckily Enright did not die while reviewing a book, and didn't
even get the books mixed up. I think I can use his own words
even for my last words on him as a book reviewer. Of all the living
writers he wrote about for me, it was probably V. S. Naipaul
whom he most consistently admired; and I would apply to
D. J. Enright the concluding words of his review (1 Oct. 1981)
of Naipaul's book *Among the Believers*:

One has one's own little vestige of faith: that the thoughts of a man of
good will, of disinterested intelligence, can somehow, in the long run,
still carry some weight.

Adding to Truth
The anthologist at work

DAVID RAWLINSON

D. J. ENRIGHT'S introduction to *Rasselas*, and his frequent recourse to its author in many different contexts, show that Samuel Johnson is one of the writers he lives with. It is not difficult to understand why he should find Johnson so congenial. Among the affinities that come to mind are an undogmatic sympathy with the downtrodden; a hatred of cant, which in Enright is often a hatred of the modern education that produces *bien pensant* attitudes of vicarious sympathy and indignation; and a keen interest in information of all kinds (Enright has reviewed a book on the history of the pig). But what draws him most of all, I believe, is Johnson's view of the nature of literary experience, the view embodied in the famous pronouncement in the Life of Cowley: 'Great thoughts are always general.' As Enright points out in the *Rasselas* introduction, this was no single truth for Johnson, who in his *Preface* to Shakespeare states: 'Nothing can please many, and please long, but just representations of general nature,' but then causes Imlac to speak of the poet's need to 'trace the changes of the human mind as they are modified by various institutions and accidental influences of climate or custom'.* Johnson is not asking that literature be a perennial reformulation of the eternal verities but that it should reflect what is important in many lives, and what is potentially important—because it is imaginable—in any life.

A modern author's consciousness of his position and role as a writer is in many ways very unlike an eighteenth-century author's, yet Johnson's presence can be felt in some of Enright's own critical convictions: for instance, in his dislike of the private, self-regarding tendency in modern verse that has 'weakened poetry as a public affair', and his preference for 'the poetry of

* Introduction to *The History of Rasselas, Prince of Abissinia*, Penguin, 1976. 18–19.

civility, passion and order';* or in his dislike of the fashionable theoretical scepticism in letters which has it that the only real certainty is that we can be sure of nothing, and which has led to the working-out of endless ramifications of that position ('those who, being able to add nothing to truth, seek for eminence from the heresies of paradox' is a favourite quotation from Johnson's *Preface*). The general anthologies Enright has produced in a manner all his own in recent years—*The Oxford Book of Death* was the first, in 1983; *The Faber Book of Fevers and Frets* followed in 1989, on a similar model; and a forthcoming *Oxford Book of Friendship*, which he is co-editing with the present writer—are an attempt to remind today's readers, in opposition to current theory and tendencies, that literature has something universal to say. Though Johnson himself never compiled an anthology, these enterprises have a Johnsonian significance. To select striking pieces of literary writing and to place them alongside striking pieces of other kinds of writing, is quietly to emphasize that literature can be read for its inspectable content, for its truth. These are different undertakings from anthologies that represent the literature of a period, such as *The Oxford Book of Seventeenth-* or *Eighteenth-Century Verse*, or of a particular literary kind or genre, such as *Ballads*. They are compendiums of the ways people have thought and felt about aspects of their lives, and include as much as possible of the variety of character, experience, gender, age, and society. Working with Enright on *Friendship* has revealed a deeply thought-out procedure.

'Friendship', as George Eliot said in *Daniel Deronda* of 'love', is 'a word of all work.' It covers an almost infinite number of possible relationships, from the casual to the lasting and committed, far more than any one writer, let alone any one description or definition, could cover. As a topic it seems even more diffuse than human reactions to death and illness, tangible facts of existence which everyone has to face. But the word nevertheless stands for something that matters in almost any life, except the lives of the misanthropic and the mad. Like 'love', it is an indispensable word. Working on the anthology, which has meant looking as far afield as possible for different experiences

---

* Introduction to *The Oxford Book of Contemporary Verse 1945–1980*, OUP, 1980. xxvii.

of friendship, still leaves an impression of common impulses and common needs, but what these are cannot properly be represented in general statements. Friendship is the subject of what one feels must be a finite number of commonplaces, but these, though easy to come by, don't represent *experiences* of friendship, and the first law of general anthologies is to avoid including too many general reflections, 'whereof a little / More than a little is by much too much'.*

'We don't need moralizing on the subject,' Enright wrote to me early on in the proceedings (the co-editing has had to be carried on from different sides of the globe); 'we have to avoid what—however well said—is mainly repetitive. Diversity of sources is essential.' And again, 'We do not want generalization, but experiences, incidents, anecdotes, anything that gives the impression of life.' Or, as Johnson in his Life of Milton once put it, in language that sounds remarkably modern, writing that has 'the freshness, raciness, and energy of immediate observation'.

As an academic probably only too used to presenting literature with explanatory, connecting discourse, I've found it a bracing business to try to find poems and extracts that can illustrate experiences of friendship tellingly but briefly, without benefit of commentary. 'Elaborate commentary is going to sink the book straight away,' wrote Enright, when I said I thought an excerpt from Plato's *Lysis* should be printed with a lengthy introductory note. What is to be used must be striking and must make itself understood, even to a reader with no knowledge of *Lysis*, who has perhaps no more than heard of Plato; and yes, a really well-chosen passage can do that. Excerpting, of course, can be difficult. 'I could explain the manner of excerpting,' Enright told me in response to some of my early efforts, 'but that would take too long.' Instead, he sent a couple of examples, each a selection of paragraphs beautifully fitted together in a way that allows the reader to follow the course of the relationship (of, say, David and Jonathan, or Fielding and Aziz), and to feel that what he has read makes an effectively shaped whole. Excerpting is not always a *pis aller*, an embarrassingly makeshift arrangement: at its best it can reveal the excerpter's sympathy with the author and a story-

---

* 1 *Henry IV*, III. ii. 72–3.

telling skill of his own. Some passages one would like to use are, of course, impossible to cut well, and Enright's experience in anthologizing makes him quick to spot these. 'The trouble with H. James,' he commented on one of my suggestions, 'is that everything depends on everything else.' James's contexts are so densely woven that no passage can stand by itself. While aiming at the broad, sweeping coverage the anthology offers, one must accept the limitations of the form and its concentration.

But I never anticipated the abundance or the variety of material that can be successfully used. When the search got under way, it soon became clear that some authors were in danger of bulking too large in the book. Shakespeare seems to present almost every kind of friendship, as it is modified by various institutions and accidental influences of climate and custom: the Renaissance student and gentleman's friendship—between ranks—of Hamlet and Horatio; the Roman friendships; the camaraderie, Elizabethan yet also of an earlier age, between Hal and Falstaff; and many others—notably between women. Friendship in Dickens could make a volume in itself. Another collection could be made from those writers, specialists in friendship, who have made of it an ethical value, usually seeing it as a stay or refuge in societies which are uncongenial or dangerous. But since I am looking at Enright's principles of anthologizing, rather than providing a preview of our Contents list, suffice it to say that one may not include too many examples from writers such as Forster, Pope, or Burns; and Dickens or Shakespeare have almost forcibly to be limited!

Johnson himself, who as Enright remarked, 'says more on friendship in fifty words than others in five thousand', could easily have swamped the collection—as apparently he could easily have swamped the earlier anthologies on death and illness. His reported remarks on friendship are all memorable: 'A man should keep his friendship in repair,' he told Reynolds, thinking of the loss of friends late in life, and again: 'to let friendship die away by negligence and silence, is certainly not wise.' Sometimes he is tart: 'How few of his friends' houses would a man choose to be at when he is sick!', and he is a very accurate observer of what he calls the most fatal disease of friendship, 'gradual decay, or dislike hourly increased by causes too slender for complaint, and

too numerous for removal.'* Johnson however is particularly
known for his strong regard for old friends, and especially for his
apparently unequal or even unlikely friendships: with Savage, with
Bet Flint the prostitute, with Levet, and with a friend from early
days, Taylor, who became a cleric and prosperous landowner, and
whose conversation sometimes bored him ('His talk is of bullocks,'
he once complained, with a glance at Ecclesiasticus). As a biographer, above all in the *Lives*, he is one of the most Shakespearean
of writers on friendship in his awareness of the many different,
sometimes surprising, ingredients that can make a friendship.

To cut down the representation of writers like these seemed
at first a sacrifice. But I had been starting from familiar ground,
and it took time, with Enright's prompting, and study of *The Oxford
Book of Death*, to realize how wide the net can and must be cast.
There are of course some famous friendships, and notorious
betrayals of friendship, that the reader will expect to find, though
it is not always easy to track down the best version, or translation.
At first the prospect of looking for non-literary sources—so
important to the undertaking—seemed rather daunting. But it
is surprising how, in a search of this kind, one thing leads to
another, and the searcher acquires an instinct for promising
openings. Letters—'Not too many literary friendships, though,'
Enright warned me; the memoirs of explorers and politicians,
people in no sense professional writers, have been particularly
fruitful. Enright has insisted on the need to include 'sincere,
human—or all too human—material' by people who may not be
very articulate but who have a right to be heard when they have
something to say that is interesting in itself, rather than by virtue
of the way they say it. *The Oxford Book of Death* is particularly rich
in such testimonies, which can have a dignity that is not reduced
when it is put in the company of the greatest writing. A confession,
a cry of hurt, a shrewdly reported incident, add to the sum of
recorded experience, and remind us of the continuities between
literature and life. Even the most unlikely source of all—an
attempt at literature—need not amount to the worst of both
worlds. There is also the rather different kind of 'ordinariness'
represented by the children's songs (recorded by the Opies) sung

---

* Boswell: I, 300; IV, 145; IV, 181, ed. Hill-Powell, OUP, 1964; and *The Idler*,
23: II, 74, Yale, 1963.

in street games that ritually enact the making and breaking of friendships. And there are the common sayings and proverbs which have at their best pungent or, at times, really delicate imaginative qualities: 'Friendship is a footprint in the sand' (African); 'When men are friendly, even water is sweet' (Chinese). Anonymous, as so often in anthologies, is one of the best authors.

Anthologies need arrangement, as natural and unelaborate as possible, for the least suspicion of didactic intent, or of mere 'book-making', will be off-putting. Readers are probably best assisted by modest categorization, though it isn't always easy to avoid some overlap of qualities. The sections partly decide themselves, and must show each piece to full advantage. Even here, the mind that Johnson says naturally loves truth, naturally loves at least some degree of order.

A belief in the general truth of literature involves a belief in the 'general reader'—a figure deemed in some specialist quarters to have been deconstructed out of existence twenty years ago, yet without whom it is hard to see how authors can write or wish to write, and without whom criticism, except as an Alexandrian self-perpetuating activity, scarcely seems possible. Enright is an example of what is now a rare thing, a scholar whose writing about a wide range of literature is accessible to a large audience, and has no feeling about it of the academy. (I have heard him say that anyone who needs an account of what a book is like would do better to turn to a journalist nowadays than to a professional critic.) He habitually shows a genuine respect for the reactions of the unprejudiced reader—it may be, often, the unprejudiced student—that it is hard to find in many contemporaries. Randall Jarrell possesses this breadth of appeal; so does Orwell, whose essays on popular forms of entertainment come to mind in reading Enright's most recent book of essays, *Fields of Vision*. It may be that writing like this will keep confidently alive the idea of the general reader during his or her absence. Enright's anthologies are part of an aim to reassert the value of literature, which Johnson asserted in his own age, and to encourage readers to expect literature to speak directly to them about what concerns them most.

Fandango with the Professor

GAVIN YOUNG

A FEW years ago, wandering back from a lunch-party somewhere near Camden tube station, I spotted a familiar figure
outside the entrance on a corner, solitary, looking skywards and
waving an umbrella in a melodramatic, Quixotic way at a passing
Jumbo 747. 'Stop!' the figure was crying. 'Give us a lift home,
will you? Oh, go on.'

'Hullo, Dennis', I said. 'Want any help?'

'The bloody thing won't stop', he complained. 'I only want a
lift to Southfields.'

We swayed about a bit in a light breeze. 'Snooty things,
aeroplanes', Dennis Enright said sadly—but not too sadly because
his lunch had obviously been better than mine. Plunging down
the tube, I looked back and saw a large airliner rapidly descending
in his direction. Surely, it wasn't going to . . . Well, I thought—I
always knew Dennis had Powers.

A Power at any rate to make everything seem livelier and
funnier—even to make me want to dance. In fact, Dennis and
I quite often round off a meal (with wine) doing what I believe
is called a *fandango*. For the benefit of inquisitive *aficionados* of
Dance, it takes four to fandango, but we have diminished the
number to two. I would describe our particular post-prandial
prance as something between Sir Roger de Coverley and Knees-
Up-Mother-Brown; the left arm is thrown up over the head, the
right arms loosely linked, and you twirl around the room (watch
the furniture!), keeping the knees well up like dray-horses in the
Lord Mayor's Show. All this summons up the blood, as another
poet once said, stiffens the sinews (you feel a pleasant ache the
next morning), and makes you ready for the next round of Vieux
Papes Moroccan Rouge, or whatever it is. As the years dwindle
down to a precious few, I sometimes wonder how much longer
we shall be able to keep up this much-hallowed ritual.

It started many years back—1965, I suppose it was—in
Singapore. Dennis Enright came hallooing round the corner of

the terrace of the 49 Shelford Road bungalow of my *Observer* colleague Dennis Bloodworth, scattering the mynah birds and apologizing for being late—although, as we were still carrying the first tonic bottles out of the kitchen and no one was expected for at least ten minutes, this was not strictly necessary. I knew a poet was awaited; I was alert for a beard and pebble glasses. I saw instead a wry, laughing version of Voltaire before me— and was to go on seeing it, luckily for me, for several years in Singapore. Often surrounded by a genial crowd of expatriate professors of the Singapore University, gathered of an evening under the trees of a delightfully ramshackle hotel of colonial vintage which, like most elderly buildings in Singapore, has since been razed to make way for some conventional skyscraping hotel. Sometimes with the Bloodworths. Or else in the large, imposing house—well, forget the odd scorpion, tarantula, or man-fearing cobra lurking beneath its mildewed boards—Dennis and Madeleine Enright rented on Cluny Hill. That was the time when Singapore was in the middle of the war of confrontation with Indonesia—President Sukarno was doing his (fortunately, hopelessly inadequate) best to break up the newly formed state of Malaysia and Singapore—and it was, for those not actually in the front-line in Borneo, quite a jolly time. Dennis, however, was at war on his own account, engaged in a running battle with the Minister of Culture, Mr S. Rajaratnam, from which in the end he was lucky, I suppose, to emerge undeported.

The crux of this battle was the Government of Singapore's campaign against 'yellow culture', (meaning, in general terms, 'western culture'). How, wondered Dennis out loud across the pints of Tiger beer, was one to define 'yellow culture'? It was a concept that seemed to range from juke-boxes to Wordsworth's daffodils, from prostitution (and we all know that nothing like *that* existed in the East before the lustful colonialists arrived there) to films, from the 'Leftist-cum-lascivious fictions of Han Suyin' to, for a time, D. J. Enright himself. The Government's efforts to build a local culture seemed to be defined only in terms of the ousting of the yellow variety. Whatever it was, local culture was to be immaculately inoffensive 'to Malays, to Chinese, to Indians, to Ceylonese, to Eurasians, to Sikhs, to Buddhists, to Christians, to Hindus, to Muslims, to atheists, to vegetarians and to carnivores'.

Despite the melodrama of it all, Dennis survived ten years in Singapore. All that is over now. After twenty-five years, Singaporeans have indeed established an identity. They don't say, 'We are Chinese', but 'We are Singaporeans'. And they are very, very pleased with themselves. Mr Rajaratnam, now retired, has let bygones be bygones. He told me very recently that he thought Mr Enright was a very good writer: one he reads and someone he would be happy to meet again. As Raja, who essentially is a nice man, was once a regular denizen of Fitzrovia in its wartime heyday, and a close friend of the celebrated Fitzrovian, Tambimuttu, that seems a most satisfactory and reasonable state of affairs.

I have always regretted missing Dennis at his most melo-dramatic, his Bangkok period. It is high time someone reprinted the novel he set there called *Insufficient Poppy*. Still, *Memoirs of a Mendicant Professor* has some excellent Bangkokiana in it. Fit, if I may make a suggestion, for a movie starring John Cleese or an English Woody Allen. (Now and again, I've glimpsed an element of Buster Keaton lurking in Dennis Enright.)

In *Memoirs* is the briefest of briefings Dennis received from the British Council before arriving in Thailand: 'Never touch a female: not even a friendly pat of encouragement.' Apparently an earlier cultural emissary had disgraced himself irrevocably by tucking a frangipani flower into some young lady's hair. Dennis, yelping with alarm, was soon having the shirt ripped out of his pants and almost off his back by a roaring bevy of surprisingly muscular Thai girl students during the rehearsal of a Council play. 'There is nothing to say they cannot lay hands on *you*', a friend unnecessarily informed him, almost too late.

Soon thereafter, a lecture Dennis delivered to a most dis-tinguished audience, which had everyone in stitches of appreci-ative glee, was described by some Council fusspot as 'deplorable', and a high-up British diplomat was heard to complain that in his view Mr Enright was 'funny-looking'. To which Dennis retorted mildly that he thought the diplomat looked a bit odd too, but he wouldn't make an issue of it. A typical response, of course. It is Dennis's irrepressibly puckish sense of humour that sticks in the mind. It runs joyously through all his novels. It contributes to making *Academic Year* a modern classic (I'm glad that Oxford University Press so classified it in its 1984 reissue) on the lines of *Hindu Holiday* and Burgess's *Malayan Trilogy*. It refuses to allow him to take anything about himself too seriously.

Even the terrible incident of the beating-up in Bangkok becomes an amusing anecdote. What happened there was that when, returning from a party, Dennis and Madeleine took the liberty of closing the open door of an empty car that was blocking the road near their house, policemen poured out of a neighbouring brothel and furiously set about them, even though no damage had been done. Dennis 'offered no resistance', but Madeleine, not so much a slave to pacifism perhaps, dealt the police lieutenant a good hard slap across the chops. In her view, the lieutenant had earned it; with great gusto, he had been kicking Dennis's lower vertebrae 'in a manner reminiscent of Thai boxing'. Easily over-powered by fifteen of Bangkok's Finest—and perhaps Tipsiest—Dennis was thrust into a communal police-cage—a peaceful and friendly place, he thought, like a crowded opium den.

The characteristic thing about the aftermath to that melodrama is the way in which, *in extremis*, Dennis's sense of proportion and humour remained intact. For he was absurdly and humiliatingly castigated by the British Embassy for having beaten up over a dozen Thai policemen without provocation and for having done who knew what damage to not only a police car (not a scratch on it) but also to Anglo–Thai relations (they continue excellent to this day). He was able easily to grin and bear the stupidity of the British Head of Chancery who sneered that the behaviour Dennis attributed to the Thai police was 'entirely out of character' (i.e. that he was lying), although any fool (any intelligent Thai, certainly) could have told him that those who find themselves in a tangle with the Bangkok police are not necessarily mischief-makers. To cap it all, the British Council Representative told Dennis he was a 'disgrace', and that he had 'dragged the name of the British Council through the mud'—adding a number of other clichés of the same sort. A sorry story. Physically painful, too. But Dennis shrugged it off, as he seems to shrug off all misfortune.

Once he even, in the cause of friendship, undertook for me the horrendous chore of wading through my journalistic writings of twenty years to produce a selection for publication. If that isn't nobility of soul, what is? He even pretends that he quite enjoyed doing it. Naturally, we both enjoyed the subsequent meal, drink—and fandango. A rather extended fandango, if I remember rightly.

What's nice about Dennis—well, apart from the poetry and the laughter—is that there's never any *fuss*; he passes everything off with a shrug and a wryly humorous passage about it in his next book. As my grandmother might have said, he has no 'side'.

Now he lives in multi-racial Southfields where the golden tip of a mosque winks at him over the tree-tops of a park. I live in hope that that wink will seduce him abroad again one day. I would love to meet him Out East again. He would stir things up. In *Insufficient Poppy*, he makes a character speak for him: 'Yes, I must curb this streak of melodrama. I've always been a moderate chap.'

Dennis Enright is one of the most moderate chaps I know. But now and again moderation needs a little bit of melodrama to set it off, don't you think?

II

In and Out of the Movement

BLAKE MORRISON

THIRTY-FIVE years on, Dennis Enright's purported association with the Movement looks like one of literary history's more whimsical jokes. How can *he* have been mixed up with *them*? How can a movement that favoured the parochial, the provincial, and the academic have recruited such an unlikely member to its ranks? Not a great joiner-in at the best of times, Enright himself must often have wondered whether a club that included Philip Larkin, John Wain, and Kingsley Amis was one which he would have voluntarily joined, however entertaining the talk at the bar. Though good company, he has always been a man apart, not the clubbable sort to get himself involved in groups, particularly that one. On the contrary, his whole career—the long years spent teaching abroad, the adventures in opium dens and outside brothels, the editorial post with a metropolitan publisher, the chancy free-lancing, the unmistakable Bohemianism of it all— seems to epitomize values which the Movement was reputed to oppose. Yet the Movement chapter of his career is an interesting one, and the question of his affiliation to this short-lived but influential 1950s literary confederacy is more complex than first appears.

His Movement associations might be traced right back to his date and place of birth, for as a working-class boy growing up in the 1920s in the Midlands and retaining left-of-centre sympathies he had the proper social, political, and generational qualifications for membership. Or they might be traced back to Cambridge, where he came under the spell of Leavis and *Scrutiny*, key influences on the Movement as a whole. Or they could be located in the acerbic and even (by his later standards) savage reviews he wrote in the late-1940s, which set the tone for subsequent Movement declarations and manifestos. Some of these reviews were bluntly *ad hominem*—his attack on Stephen Spender's volume *Ruins and Visions*, for instance ('blatantly bankrupt . . . only half the title is really apposite, I'm afraid'), and his demolition

job on the Neo-Apocalypse poetry of Henry Treece (a 'kind
of surrealist Bogeyland'). But other reviews took on a whole
generation and cultural climate, notably his piece on 'The Significance of *Poetry London*', which accused Tambimuttu's magazine
and others like it of 'conducting a wholesale perversion of both
the taste of the poetry-reader and the talent of the poetry-writer'.
Such articles have the impatient air of a young man wanting to
kill off the old guard, if not quite sure how to usher in the new.

But it was a praising notice by Enright which was to have the
most lasting consequences for the Movement. In 1951 Philip
Larkin sent out his privately printed collection *XX Poems* for
review, and was greeted with a deafening silence, one which he
later explained must have been the consequence of his having
failed to take into account that the price of postage had just gone
up. But he did receive at least one review—by D. J. Enright in
his capacity as reviewer for the Catholic periodical *The Month*.
Enright had had the book drawn to his attention by Charles
Madge and wrote that Larkin's poetry showed 'a respect for
language which is beginning to look old-fashioned these days;
he persuades words into being poetry, he does not bully them.
This little pamphlet whets the appetite: it is to be hoped that some
publisher will take the hint.' Larkin and Enright exchanged letters
after this, and on one occasion Charles Madge nearly brought
them together in Birmingham, where Enright was then teaching,
but 'Larkin's shyness prevented it'. It was to be some years before
they met—and some years before a publisher, and then only a
small press one, George Hartley, took Enright's hint. None the
less, it's significant that the sole encouragement Larkin had, in
the lean years between *The North Ship* and his appearances in the
magazine *Listen*, had come from a poet with whom (and by
whom) he was eventually to be anthologized.

How Enright came to put together his 1955 anthology *Poets
of the 1950's*, and why it bore such a resemblance to Robert
Conquest's *New Lines* the following year, has been a matter of
much speculation and not a little accusation of ganging up.
Conquest was, in fact, the one Movement poet Enright had met,
the two having publicly praised each other's work and privately
exchanged letters. Enright admits that he wrote to Conquest from
Japan, telling him of his intentions and asking him for advice
about who to put in his anthology; the poets they eventually

anthologized coincide exactly except for Thom Gunn, whom
Enright would have included, he says, had he known his work.
But Enright, it turns out, already had his list of eight poets
independently, before Conquest offered any suggestions, and
he made no later adjustments: there was no sinister take-over
of British poetry. How could there be, in any case? Enright's
anthology was printed and published in Japan, and was intended
to provide a guide to Japanese teachers and students as to what
was happening in England; it wasn't a call to arms, let alone
an act of provocation, but a cheap edition selling in academic
bookshops at the equivalent of three shillings, and such wider
celebrity as it had came later and retrospectively.

If Enright's reviewing and anthologizing explain how he came
to acquire the Movement label, his poetry and fiction tell a quite
different story about his affinities. It is not that it is hard to find
evidence of family resemblances—the Jim Dixon-like traits of
Packet in *Academic Year* and *Heaven Knows Where*, which also
anticipate the campus fiction of Lodge and Bradbury; the grittily,
smokily realistic provincial setting of his Black Country poems in
The Laughing Hyena; the controlled, almost jaunty reasonableness
and even ratiocination (under great duress) of 'Death of a Child';
the jokey fondness (always the right side of patronizing) for
recounting student examination or essay howlers; the ironies and
wrynesses and sceptical undertones; the capacity, explored in a
poem of that title, for 'saying no'. But Enright's nay-saying
isn't the bluff kind of commonsense, the having-no-truck-with-
pretentious-nonsense, that one gets in Amis or Wain, or sometimes
even Larkin, but a refusal caught up with the burdens of modern
history:

> Some virtue here, in this speech-stupefied inane,
> To keep it short.
> However cumbrous, puffed and stretched the pain—
> To say no more than, No.
>
> Virtue (or only decency) it would have been,
> But—no.
> I dress that death's-head, all too plain, too clean,
> With lots of pretty lengths of saying,
>
> No.

(CP, 44)

A strong temptation to say 'yes' insinuates itself everywhere in Enright, and if generous affirmation is resisted in 'Saying No' it stems not from meanness of spirit but from a sense that, when words have become tarnished and unreliable, curt negation may be the first step towards building a better world. This is perhaps only another way of asserting that Enright's poems, much more than most of the Movement's, rise to the challenge that a poet be concerned with his time and place. In Enright's case, this can sometimes mean beginning with other times and other places, of putting the present in context, of getting here from there. (A natural process for him, since while most Movement poets were academics but ill-read, Enright is widely read but not academic.) He does this, for example, in 'The Laughing Hyena, after Hokusai', which sings the praises of that ugly face, 'cavalier of evil' (a typically rich but unflashy ambiguity): alongside the 'sententious phantoms' of the present, all smiles and double messages, the laughing hyena has at any rate the virtue of its vices: 'It, at least, / Knows exactly why it laughs.'

The Movement poets were celebrated for their return to formal symmetry and syntactical clarity, after British poetry had been roughed up by Dylan Thomas. Here again, Enright doesn't quite fit: the clothes are altogether too tight for him. There is a bagginess about his poems, a loose plain-speakingness, which sometimes militates against their artistry, or more precisely their music: he is not a poet, like Larkin or Hardy, whose cadences one finds oneself carrying around. But there is something authenticating and Lawrentian about this, too—as if the poet can't bear to let his eye stray from the subject, however unbearable it might have been to focus on it in the first place; or as if getting your ideas in order is more important than finding the perfect rhyme (rhyme, in any case and for that reason, being something Enright uses only sparingly). In 'Excusing the Cicadas' Enright defends the habitual appearance of those creatures in *haikus*: they are 'the monstrous life / Those seventeen syllables cannot embrace'. His own stanzas, too, are thick with monstrous creatures, whether beggars or atom-bombs, which have forced their way, against decorum, on to the page.

Enright is famous for his compassion, his close-up poems about the underprivileged and underpaid and undernourished. Such a quality is often spoken of condescendingly, as if it were some sort of failure of self-control. But his compassion isn't cosy or inhibiting or incapacitating since it's never a matter of doling out pity. For him, taking a good look at the bad often leads to a larger view of the worse: Hiroshima, the concentration camps, political revolt, totalitarian regimes all quietly find their way into his books. Not so quietly, either, if we're listening properly. The easy colloquialism that runs through such poems is deceptive: it gives us the illusion that we are paddling in the shallows when the water is already over our heads. The way these poems shuffle on to the centre-stage of history as if by accident is what makes them troubling, and it's also part of the reason they make trouble for themselves and for their author. It was never, I believe, a specific poem that got him into hot water with a foreign government, though poems sent home from Bangkok to be published in the *New Statesman* seem to have upset his nervous employers, the British Council, rather than the easy-going Thais. None the less, perhaps his experience of the dangers of words has been enough to make him, in 1989, firm in his support of Salman Rushdie.

Movement poets don't want to cause trouble, on the whole, and it's in this respect more than any other that Enright is a writer apart—his own man by being so concerned for other men, regardless of the consequences. Of all Dennis's witticisms, the one I like best comes from a letter responding to some questions from the American critic, William van O'Connor. No, he says, 'I haven't seen the phrase "obsessive humanity" applied to my poetry. But I wouldn't object to it. What else is there to be obsessed with?'

'The Thunder of Humanity'
D. J. Enright's Liberal Imagination

DOUGLAS DUNN

YOU COULD tell that a state of mind was on its way out when it became fashionable to stick 'wishy-washy' in front of 'liberal'. It had begun to suffer from worthiness. A mentality that included a wide variety of practitioners, it looked as if it represented the *absence* of definition, whether politically, culturally, or intellectually; it looked too good to be true. Its political demise was more visible than any other. Ethical seriousness, intelligence, and humour had to be shown to the door by a re-energized Conservative Party whose 'liberals' did not survive for very long—they were called 'wets', an epithet rather similar to 'wishy-washy'. Militants on the Left went in for name-calling of the same pejorative order, and if something like a liberal mentality on the defensive suppressed stridency and rancour within the Labour Party, it has always looked more like an electoral strategy. One can always believe otherwise, of course.

To many, poetry seems ill at ease with the liberal intellect. Eccentricities, extremes, and the unpredictable fit poetry better, or so it is alleged, than the discriminatory and the reasonable. 'Ratiocination drives Poetry away', wrote Goethe, 'but she is a friend of what is reasonable.' However, ratiocination is not the issue. Feeling and intelligence are at stake here, the friendship between Poetry and the reasonable. Their affinity might be elective as much as natural, for, like many states of virtuous concord, an affable relationship with one might mean that you don't see as much as you'd like of another, whose friends will accuse you of having made the wrong alliance. In D. J. Enright's poetry, for example, founded as it is on a liberal mentality, imagination plays a different role than in poetry where reasonable feelings take second place in deciding what is said and how.

As it develops through his first two or three books, Enright's style seeks to identify itself as on the side of clarity and plainness. It tends to the laconic and relishes brevity and the aphoristic.

Increasingly, fat stanzas favoured for their intricate regularity, opulent figurativeness, ornamental diction, and anything associated with the prolix, will come to feel as if banished from his repertoire or never to have crossed his mind as possibilities. 'One represents an obscure and well-known poet', he says in 'The Peaceful Island' where he throws stones at a row of empty bottles. Other targets for his good-natured vandalism include a pimp, a 'flinty industrialist', and someone 'expert in traditions and hopes for war'.

Attention paid to lives beyond his own feels like the compelling reason for the attitudes and stylistic formations of his poetry. In these earlier books the poems are quite self-consciously about facing up to reality and achieving a viable angle of approach to recent history and topical, observable scenes and people. In 'Life and Letters' he withdraws from the temptation to exploit compassion for the victims of history. 'And history—my own—oh nothing more portentous—/Pressed me both ways', is followed by a gesture in imagery that tries to invalidate Romantic grandiloquence: 'The near stars smelt of jasmine, and the moon—that huge fallafel—faintly of garlic.' Wittily, slyly, Enright has it both ways; as an antithesis, the line holds a lyrical perception and its wilfully demotic counterpart. 'For history—in the smallest sense— had fallen about me', continues his fastidious qualifications, stressing an attempted reasonableness that does not gainsay a lyric impulse—a sensible lyricism—and prepares for the poem's final lines:

Which is why I try to write lucidly, that even I
Can understand it—and mildly, being loath to
  face the fashionable terrors,
Or venture among sinister symbols, under ruin's shadow.
Once having known, at an utter loss, that utter
  incomprehension
—Unseen, unsmelt, the bold bat, the cloud of jasmine,
Truly out of one's senses—it is unthinkable
To drink horror from ink, to sink into the darkness of words,
Words one has chosen oneself. Poems, at least,
Ought not to be phantoms.

                                                              (CP, 14)

Post-War disillusionment, together with the mercy of small pleasures, seem obvious sources of the feeling in 'Life and Letters'.

In a more general sense, what the poem rejects can be suggested
by quoting four lines from Heine's 'Believe Me!' if only to point
out that Enright's quarrel with poetic irresponsibility is a recurrent
one:

> But songs and stars and flowers by the ton,
> Or eyes and moons and springtime sun,
> No matter how much you like such stuff,
> To make a world they're just not enough.*

Doubtless, Enright's strategy accorded to a considerable extent
with how the literary times were tending in the shape of the
Movement. Working abroad, however, as Enright chose or
was fated to do for much of his life—Egypt, Japan, Germany,
Thailand, and Singapore—detached him from at least the more
crucial of those characteristically English restraints that fudge
the point where poetry, society, and politics meet. History 'in
the smallest sense' or history as 'portentous' fits in comfortably
with English attitudes to ambition—'We were the Descendancy',
he writes in 'Entrance Visa', 'Hurt but not surprised.' More
than any other poet of his generation, he has been consistent
in confronting social and political subjects with passionate
intelligence and abundant feeling. Indeed, his work feels awkward
in the context of the Movement, even if it shares in common with
Larkin's poetry (for instance) a few general principles of style and
attitude. Larkin's world, however, is astoundingly narrow when
compared to Enright's international reach of Englishness. It would
be unjust to say that he is more generous than Larkin; he is more
generous than just about everybody.

  Experience of Japan would leave Enright certain that 'Poems,
at least, ought not to be phantoms', but any lingering trace
of history as portentous or embarrassingly massive was to be
modified by the need to reply to what he witnessed. His Japanese
poems are populated by underdogs, beggars, typhoon victims,
Hiroshima's casualties, bar-girls, and a suicidal shoeshine boy.
It is a country in receipt of 'Edible Aid', with a strong presence
of poverty and 'the monstrous life' that the seventeen syllables
of *haiku* cannot express through its redundant preciosity. Sad,
sorrowful poems that they are, they have touches of lightness,

---

* Trans. Hal Draper, *The Complete Poems of Heinrich Heine* (OUP, 1982).

of a liberal sanity, or sometimes a sturdy metre, that enliven them in such a way as to place them on the side of conscience and responsibility, but at the same time they are complicated by Enright's temperamental hedonism. As much as anything else it might be a matter of tone:

> Only one subject to write about: pity.
> Self-pity: the only subject to avoid.
> How difficult to observe both conditions!
>
> .   .   .   .
>
> But make no mistake. Suffering exists, and most of it
>   is not yours.
> Good acts are achieved, as good poems are. Most of them
>   not by you.
>   ('How right they were, the Chinese poets', CP, 22)

Some of them even have a grumbling, grim humour—'Displaced Person Looks at a Cage-Bird', or 'The Pied Piper of Akashi'. A poem like 'Broken Fingernails' remarks on its own methods while pictorializing a scene:

> A shabby old man is mixing water with clay.
> If that shabby old man had given up hope
> (He is probably tired: he has worked all day)
> The flimsy house would never have been built.
>
> If the flimsy house had never been built
> Six people would shiver in the autumn breath.
> If thousands of old men were sorry as you
> Millions of people would cough themselves to death.
>
> (In the town the pin-ball parlours sing like cicadas
> Do not take refuge in some far-off foreign allusion
> (In the country the cicadas sing like pin-ball parlours)
> Simply remark the clay, the water, the straw,
>   and a useful person.
>   (CP, 22)

Of a shoeshine boy who wanted to die because he had a headache:

> The policeman took it down, adding that
>   you were quite
> Alone and had no personal belongings, other than a headache.

'Elsewhere the great ones have their headaches, too', he continues,

> As they grapple with those notable tongue-twisters
> Such as Sovereignty and Subjection.
> But they were not talking about you,
> Kazuo, who found rat poison cheaper than aspirin.
> ('The Short Life of Kazuo Yamamoto', CP, 17–18)

His idiom is undeceived; it conspires with what he observes to show that he is neither reconciled to bruising topicality nor Parnassianly detached. His acceptance of life is plain, ordinary, and critical in its recognition of human suffering; his detachment is an enabling artifice that creates a sympathetic angle of observation, a literary lens that makes it possible for him to record the scene while leaving room for comment. 'The poor are always with us. Only they can find a value in the new', for example, is pretty insolent in its implications as well as bald and laconic. 'Happy New Year', however, shows Enright close to his best, supple, almost funny in his depiction of a New Year encounter with a banker who bewails ' "A hard year for Japan" '.

> He clapped me by the hand, he led me to his bright
>   new house.
> He showed his ancient incense burners, precious
>   treasures, cold and void.
> His family too he showed, drawn up in columns,
>   and his fluttering spouse.
> We bowed and wept together over the grim new year.
>
> I walked away, my head was full of yen, of falling yen.
> I saw the others with their empty pockets,
> Merry on the old year's dregs, their mouths
>   distilled a warm amen!
>
> The poor are always with us. Only they can find
>   a value in the new.
> They are the masters of their fourpenny kites
> That soar in the open market of the sky.
> Whatever wrongs await, they still preserve some rites.
> (CP, 19–20)

Anachronistic or traditional Japan is contrasted with 'the new', and 'the others with their empty pockets' with the banker whose 'saké-smelling tear suffused his reddened eye'. It is remarkably simple, but also subtle, casual-seeming, though pruned to the bare bones of a narrative. 'And yet and yet' in the first stanza probably echoes the celebrated *haiku* by Issa written on the death of his only son, which acknowledges the limitations of Buddhist acceptance, and perhaps also of art and poetry:

> The world of dew
> Is a world of dew and yet,
> And yet.

That risky pun—'some rites'—is a long way from the manners of Japanese poetry. Its ruefulness feels peculiarly English; it is characteristic of Enright's injurious flippancy, the way in which he can rearrange the reader's expectation by guiding a dispiriting subject into humorous moments. Perhaps it is largely a matter of temperament that he can do this convincingly. In any case his writing depends on a personality more interesting than that of a man intent on telling stories of misfortune and poking you in the eye with pictures of deprivation.

His idiom becomes more grimly waggish in 'The Monuments of Hiroshima'. Here his ruefulness makes him seem a *farceur* of apocalypse, but speaking on behalf of atomized victims. 'Little of peace for them to rest in', he says, 'less of them to rest in peace.' The skin creeps, not just at the fact, but the bleak joke of it, just as in the first two lines the English clichés of death feel as if they are being admonished at the same time as their demotic humour is savoured.

> The roughly estimated ones, who do not sort well
>   with our common phrases,
> Who are by no means eating roots of dandelion,
>   or pushing up the daisies.

The next verse works with something like a a dignified, negative lyricism, winking, perhaps, at graveyard poetry in the process, raising the tone:

> The more or less anonymous, to whom no human idiom
>   can apply,
> Who neither passed away, or on,
>   nor went before, nor vanished on a sigh.
>
> (CP, 19)

Worthy gestures, big constructions, are diminished in proportion to how the dignity of the dead could be restored were there anything of them left to fit the average expectations of a coffin. Or not restored. Irony, after all, is irony—the creating of mental space within which a considerable degree of doubt is possible.

The oppositional sentiments of Enright's Japanese poems were probably too local for their force to be felt by some English readers of the time. In *Memoirs of a Mendicant Professor*, Enright stated that 'The blank unbridgeable chasm between an exquisite sensitivity towards the arts and a stolid insensitivity towards human suffering was just a little more than a Western softie like myself could accommodate.'* But if the immediate subjects of these poems are Japanese that does not suggest that we should fail to attend to the uninsular Englishness of a poetry already benefiting from an affection for Brecht and Cavafy as well as an expertly idiosyncratic interpretation of recent poets such as Lawrence, Auden, and MacNeice, perhaps even Kipling (those long lines, for example). There is something indigenously English about Enright's wit. His clownish, ironic sorrowfulness, his melancholy and his distrust of it, would seem to me to have a touch of Warwickshire about them. I can't help but quote a remark of Ford Madox Ford's from his *A History of Our Own Times*: 'a man must have a certain insularity if he is to live. Given that your glass is reasonably large it is out of your own glass that you had better drink.' What you put into your glass, of course, is entirely up to you.

Enright's hedonism is inseparable from his compassion. In *Memoirs of a Mendicant Professor* he wrote of Japanese bar-girls that

* *Memoirs of a Mendicant Professor*, 38. That was in Japan. Enright then proceeds to indulge in a spot of tetchiness: 'But in England things were very different of course, it was not people who suffered there, it was the arts and the intellect. So my mutterings seemed strangely incongruous, an outburst of Kulturbolschevismus which left Apeneck Amis looking like a museum curator. When I pleaded my case with Donald Davie (who had reviewed my Japanese poems) he remarked that it was queer and not right that disagreement about a body of poems should resolve itself into conflicting diagnoses about what was wrong with English or Japanese society, since that was the kind of thing which should concern us as intellectuals but not as poets. Yes, it was queer. I should have written the poems in Japanese, or else written them about England. Or better still, written aboutlessly.'

(See Donald Davie's essay, p. 150, later in this book, where he returns to the question. Ed.)

'These girls seemed to me instances of the most arrant, most heart-breaking wastage of human goodness which I had encountered outside books'. In 'Tea Ceremony', after dismissing Zen otherness, he takes sides with 'life-size people, / Rooted in precious little, without benefit of philosophy'. (Like MacNeice, he reloads clichés: 'Beyond the bamboo fence . . .'; 'precious little'; 'without benefit of . . .'.)

> So pour the small beer, Sumichan. And girls,
>   permit yourselves a hiccup, the thunder
> Of humanity. The helpless alley is held by
>   sleeping beggars under
> Their stirring beards, and the raw fish curls
> At the end of the day, and the hot streets cry
>   for the careless scavengers.
>
> (CP, 20–1)

These are exhilarating lines. Their rhetoric directs them into unusual literary territory—a mixture of a toast, an insult to ceremonial, advocacy, and the evocation of the circumstances of somewhere else—this latter element is not 'exotic', it is just interesting. 'Akiko San' elegizes a bar-girl and is as affirmative as that passage from 'Tea Ceremony'. However, the invention of 'a modest Jerusalem', and later 'Jerusalem' itself, indicate an affectionate defensiveness that rubs close to the sentimental. It is possible to agree with this poem and at the same time regret that it has stepped outside the lucid moral circumference of Enright's other Japanese poems. In 'Akiko San' he is all wish and feeling. Its notes are sweet, but the more acidic tenderness, the stringency and ironic hygiene of the poems surrounding it, isolate 'Akiko San' as a different kind of poem, leaving the impression that its whole-heartedness does not suit him, and that a different kind of equally whole-hearted commitment does.

Enright's Japanese poems have preoccupied me because they are so good. They are close to the thing itself as the fright of the world was in the 1950s. They show a 'liberal imagination' at full cry and dedicated to the reality of the moment:

> And I, like other listeners,
> See my stupid sadness as a common thing.
> And being common,
> Therefore something rare indeed.

The puffing vendor, surer than a trumpet,
Tells us we are not alone.
Each night that same frail midnight tune
Squeezed from a bogus flute,
Under the noise of war, after war's noise,
It mourns the fallen, every night,
It celebrates survival—
In real cities, real houses, real time.
　　('The Noodle-Vendor's Flute', CP, 32–3)

That an Englishman should have written about such feelings in
the 1950s is not just exceptional, but, I believe, unique, given their
particularity, and, that being the case, their universal extension.
How impertinent of a poet, and an Englishman too, to put his
finger on the pulse of a decade! And the vulgarity of it, the
temerity, to write as if the world and its societies mattered more
than poetry!—Why, that's what we expect of *foreigners*, like
Camus, or Brecht! What insulting presumptuousness, to speak
of 'real cities, real houses, real time', and yet he's talking about
Japan! Talk about selling the pass? This man sells it *repeatedly*!

Discussions of recent English poetry have been prone to what
Lionel Trilling described as 'irritable mental gestures which seek
to resemble ideas'. Enright's absence from an intimate literary
scene was therefore fortunate, an enabling circumstance, even
if—especially in Singapore—survival at times depended on
'silence, exile, cunning, hysterics, sloth, "low posture" (as the
sociologists call it) and simple-mindedness . . .' In any case,
England, 'that nest of stinging birds', has always distrusted poetry
when it touches on politics, a proximity which liberalism in
literature takes for granted—or, in Trilling's words, 'the inevitable
intimate, if not always obvious connexion between literature and
politics'. And yet if there was an emotional topicality in Larkin's
poetry of the same period, supported by the realism of his urban
imagery, that seems to be about as far as average taste was
prepared to go. A less selfish, more damaging, more critical
present-dayness always seems to court the suspicion of the
English reader.

But like most writers of a liberal tendency Enright has been
apolitical, a purveyor of benevolent anarchy. 'Political scientists,
the morticians of our age', he says in *Memoirs of a Mendicant
Professor*. It is not the remark of someone who takes politics

seriously; or, rather, it is the opinion of a man who takes the consequences of politics very seriously indeed. Unlike most English poets he has elicited official wrath. His chastening experience in Singapore, and being beaten up by policemen in Bangkok (which left him sensitive to the 'faint but still perceptible odour of rubber truncheons') can be supposed to have stiffened his highly agreeable gift for speaking back, polishing, indeed, the brass of his neck. His writing certainly takes on a more hazardous immediacy. 'It's not the easy life you think, this sanity', he says, beginning 'Doctor Doctor', a tart but also funny portrayal of an expatriate predicament:

> Look—
> The streets fall down, and blame you
> In cracked voices for expatriate indifference.
>
> .   .   .   .
>
> Extending your feet to a baby bootblack
> You perceive your shoes have been abducted.
> Bar-girls will relieve you of the exact amount.
> Do not argue. It is the exact amount.
>
> .   .   .   .
>
> (You think it is easy, all this sanity?
> Try it. It will send you mad.)
>
> .   .   .   .
>
> On the walls, eastern godlings spew into pewter pots.
> You have knocked everybody's drink over:
> Everybody is drinking double brandy.
>
> (CP, 75–6)

A freer verse with more room for impish humour forms an important element in the difference between the idiom of his poems of the Sixties onwards and the metrical style of his Japanese poems. Brecht and Cavafy seem to have been sources of guidance here, but influences explain less than we tend to believe in the determination of how and why a poet modifies his style. 'Why?' is in any case a more interesting question to put and the answer seems to be a simple need to reply to a climate of opinion which placed Enright in a position of alleged notoriety.

Yet it is noticeable in the poem that the particularity of its subject coincides with an ability to universalize it. 'Doctor Doctor' continues:

> Do not complain.
> In this world you have no alibi.
> You disagreed with history, now history disagrees
>   with you.
> 'Guilty' — plead this — 'guilty but sane.'

Although still undeceived, Enright's poetry now becomes disenchanted; its purpose is to disenchant, but its scepticism and wit keep hopelessness at bay.

> Nothing human is alien to me.
> Except knives, and maybe the speeches
> Of politicians in flower.
>
> ('Political Meeting', CP, 68)

> In this vale of teargas

> Should one enter a caveat,
> Or a monastery?
>
> ('Unlawful Assembly', CP, 88–9)

> You need defeat's sour
> Fuel for poetry.
> Its motive power
> Is powerlessness.
>
> ('Cultural Freedom', CP, 92)

> The more rational you are
> (What you have paid for
> You will expect to obtain
> Without further payment)
> The less your chances of remission.
>
> ('How Many Devils Can Dance on the Point . . .', CP, 111–12)

With 'Prime Minister', 'Meeting the Minister for Culture', 'What became of What-was-his-name?', and 'Come to Sunny S' Enright can be seen sailing close to the wind. He has described the first of these poems as 'harmless', and 'a not unsympathetic general study' — but we should not be taken in — 'applicable to almost any Prime Minister of any newly independent country who finds himself under the necessity of issuing orders for the arrest of the young men so recently his comrades in the struggle against the imperialist power'. Although pirated by dissidents operating outside Singapore the poem did not land Enright in trouble. It is still uncompromising in its treatment of the psychology of political ruthlessness. Psychological insight is also the strength of 'What became of What-was-his-name?'

> Funny,
> After three years
> A new generation hangs around the place,
> Hardly one of them has heard of M—.
> It makes you feel your age.
>
> (CP, 80–2)

But as Enright says, the argument of his poem about a political prisoner backfired. 'All I had managed to do, it seemed, was to encourage a man to stay in prison.' M—, Enright thought, wasn't the sort to accept prison as a 'favourite freedom', which is sometimes the choice of professional martyrs.

> He seemed to me a food and drink man.
> But he must have done something very bad.
> The papers said nothing about it.

Actual circumstances and the cast of the poem are reminiscent of Brecht in poems like 'The Burning of the Books'. Increasingly, Enright devoted his imagination to parable-making or the invention of witty narratives or poems of plain speaking. Liberalism, however, is seen as having backfired too. M—'s fate, Enright says, serves as 'an epitome of the liberal in the world as it is'. M— chose to go to jail, and stay there, rather than recant, even when imprisonment condemned him to total ineffectiveness.

. . . the liberal, the man who believes in truth and justice, or in fairness and decency, he cannot be trusted. He is the enemy of all doctrine — it was his sort of person who said 'there is no general doctrine which is not capable of eating out our morality if unchecked by the deep-seated habit of direct fellow-feeling with individual fellow-men' — and every politician's hand will be against him. His politics were shifty to begin with and they will continue to be so. He sees good in practically everything, he sees bad in practically everything; he grants you your point, and then expects you to grant him a point in return. He cannot be relied on, he is undisciplined, unrealistic, ungrateful, and he pampers his little private conscience. Prison is his proper place.*

Enright is describing his own convictions in that marvellously nimble passage of simmering irony. Has any other contemporary British poet been so articulate in defence of the humanity which we all claim to believe in? I doubt it. Yet his sociable, garrulous, inventive, often funny poetry disdains the sombre garments of 'commitment' as that notion has been re-processed and over-exposed until it now lies down in a state of exhaustion. His commitment is diffuse; it is the weather of his poetry, and there is a satisfying amount of it. He is a poet who welcomes 'little mercies, / A something to be going on with'; he is also the poet of 'Dreaming in the Shanghai Restaurant' — 'I would like to be that elderly Chinese gentleman',

> He is interested in people, without wanting to
>   convert them or pervert them.
> He eats with gusto, but not with lust;
> And he drinks, but is not drunk.
> He is content with his age, which has always suited
>   him.
> When he discusses a dish with the pretty waitress,
> It is the dish he discusses, not the waitress.
>
> .   .   .   .
>
> I guess that for him it is peace in his time.
> It would be agreeable to be this Chinese gentleman.
>   (CP, 59–60)

He is also the poet of *The Terrible Shears* and *Instant Chronicles*, an autobiographical poet who explains his life, recollects, sifts his memory for stories, and the poet of *Paradise Illustrated* and *A Faust Book*, a learned poet, a literary poet, but one who wears his erudition with playful lightness.

Personally, I believe Enright's poems written in Egypt and the Far East to be his best. What he lived and felt in Japan, Thailand, and Singapore, matters of daily witness, offered him a grimmer, more dramatic range of subjects than England afforded, and with them a more testing challenge to his tough-mindedness. Some

---

* DJE, *Memoirs of a Mendicant Professor*, 174–5.

sort of literary and personal release might also have been triggered off by being 'far from the home where the Beowulf roams'. Circumstances in the Far East made it natural that his poetry should reflect political realities. In *The Terrible Shears*, his attempt to write about social class is largely unconvincing. His poems set in the Far East are simply more ambitious, more sustained, more passionate than the snippets of *The Terrible Shears*.

To end by stating that Enright's Eastern poems are his best is not enough. They stand among the best poems of their time. Their gestures are exemplary. He faces the affronts of the world and does more than stay sane, but increases in sanity; and he perfects a style that is equal to dramatizing the emotional and intellectual experiences of witnessed poverty, hardship, authoritarian governments, unprincipled manœuvres of one kind or another, and the dismal fates which people are prone to have imposed upon them. All this, too, is conducted by a personality that is attracted to life's enjoyments. Perhaps his poetry is best read as testimony on how to stay sane in the world as it was, and as it is. 'Things aren't what they were, of course: they never were.'

The Accents of Enright

WILLIAM WALSH

D. J. ENRIGHT'S long career, devoted above all to poetry, began with a modest act of rejection. He was, as we have already been reminded, associated with the 'Movement' in the Fifties, but in his *Oxford Book of Contemporary Verse* he is as hospitable to the anti-Movement Apocalyptics and Mavericks as he is to the members of the Movement itself. Not that these poets had much in common, no concerted programme or destination: nothing perhaps, but an attitude of rejection and the word 'no'.

> After so many (in so many places) words,
> It came to this one, No.
> Epochs of parakeets, of peacocks, of paradisiac birds—
> Then one bald owl croaked, No.
>
> (CP, 44)

In Enright's case, the word 'No' registered a vote against many things: against the gentility which had oppressed him as a boy of his class and time. It meant, on the positive side, a decision in favour of a sensibility more in keeping with the reality of the times. The new sensibility was to be agile and fluent, and the voice through which it would be projected would be casual and intelligently modulated. The inflatedly poetic was out; in were a modesty of manner, a quiet decency of feeling, and an utterance more closely fitted to the contours of contemporary speech.

An act of rejection invariably contains elements of what is rebuffed, and in Enright's early poems we can see, alongside the new endeavour, an irresistible romantic warmth and over-cerebral energy. The level of technical skill is astonishingly mature. To take a less well-known early poem than the brilliant 'Laughing Hyena', here are lines from 'A Winter Scene (Hendrick Avercamp, Dutch School)', which display a mature control of imagist clarity and an appropriate gliding rhythm, together with an unabashed romantic pleasure in movement itself:

The tree uproots herself to join this rout,
About to lift her skirts; the birds look nervous—

Well they might: an easy hundred chubby burghers
Skip and skate and waltz and trip and fall;
And one man seems to drown, but no one cares at all.

                                        (CP, 10)

Poems inspired by art will be rare, and only faintly presage the
authentic Enright sensibility which was one increasingly committed
to a personal engagement with reality. In Enright, this sense of
reality is increasingly defined by exact and lucid detail. Already we
can see this at work in a remarkable early poem, 'The Chicken's
Foot'. As this poem is not in the Collected volume, I feel justified
in quoting it in full (it comes in the Middle East section of
The Laughing Hyena):

The Chicken's Foot

A weird choir sang through the huge house: a dozen draughts
Fluted about the stair-rails, and up the lift-shafts rose
                        the sea's deep voices:
The walls vibrated keenly, each brick wailed its little song:
The tempest rose and fell, transmuted to this sad and nervous music.

Outside sad Arabs hugged their handcarts, veils or babies, fleeing
With uncertain motions among the mud and puddles: scraps of paper
Rose weakly this and that way, fell wet to earth, under the naked
                        slipping feet:
Fruitsellers shrieked their prices in unusual anguish: the wind
Ravished the cabbage of its leaves, the client of his tall tarbush:
Outside the great wind sailed untamed, at liberty, unframed to art.

At the end of this little street, unnamed, unfamed, a street
                        that one might take
Unseeingly, to cheat the wind or to avoid one's friends,
A street like others, unduly ravaged by the tempest's tail,
Vulnerable to nature's riots though inured to man's—
At the bottom of this fluttered street, flat in the choked gutter,
I saw the neat claws, the precise foot, of a chicken—
Bright yellow leggings, precious lucid nails, washed by the waters,
Victim of our bellies, memorable sermon, oh murdered singing throat,
Confronting the battered traveller, fingers spread in admonition.

The wind howled louder in derision: oh literary pedestrian,
Small bankrupt moralist, oh scavenger of the obvious symbol!
But entering the huge house, where the wind's scattered voices,
Hot with insidious history, chill with foreboding, surged through
                                        my body,
The chicken's foot, naked and thin, still held my mind between its
                                        claws—
The cleanest thing, most innocent, most living, of that morning.

This is a distinctly literary poem, full of extravagance, relying on
traditional alliteration, and rhetoric even, until the poet, bounding
along a short cut ('to cheat the wind or to avoid one's friends')
is stopped short by the sight of the chicken's foot in the gutter.
Even then, self-mockery checks any tendency to sentimentality
('oh literary pedestrian'), and the third verse cools the romanticism
with a touch of astringency and serves to remind us of the
complexities of the poet's personality. In this poem, 'the point
of repose in the picture, the point of movement in us' (as he put
it when looking at Hokusai's 'Laughing Hyena') is the accurate
definition of the central symbol, in this case, 'the precise foot,
of a chicken'. Such a purpose requires of the poet an aversion
from the irrational and a bias towards intelligibility.

   Many of the early poems rely on such ends and means. They
also belong to that genre to which British writers have contributed
so much, the literature of travel. Enright's poems of this kind are
illumined by the perception of a gifted observer, whose first
sight is unblurred, and whose second is subtly deductive; he is
practised at putting himself in a position to make an eloquent
notation of the human scene. The common characteristic of
his observations of place is to show 'place' as stained or even
saturated by the particulars of human history and the effects of
human presence. No nature poet, he. In Egypt, Germany, Japan,
and Bangkok the examples are everywhere. How acrid the scent
of Bangkok, for instance, blending brutality and gentleness in
'The Burning of the Pipes':

     Who would imagine they were government property?—
     Wooden cylinders with collars of silver, coming
     From China, brown and shiny with sweat and age.
     Inside them were banks of dreams, shiny with
     Newness, though doubtless of time-honoured stock.
     They were easy to draw on: you pursed your lips

As if to suckle and sucked your breath as if to
Sigh: two skills which most of us have mastered.

The dreams themselves weren't government property.
Rather, the religion of the people. While the state
Took its tithes and the compliance of sleepers.
Now a strong government dispenses with compliance,
A government with rich friends has no need of tithes.

        .   .   .   .

A surprise to find they were government property
—Sweat-brown bamboo with dull silver inlay—
As they blaze in thousands on a government bonfire,
In the government park, by government order!
The rice crop is expected to show an increase,
More volunteers for the army, and navy, and
Government service, and a decrease in petty crime.

                                        (CP, 54–5)

Enright has a knack of suddenly infusing banal or bureaucratic
language with another amazing life. Occasionally in these poems
of place the aim is awry, and the intention subverted by the shock
of a contrast between the comic, commonplace phrases and
the enormity of what is commemorated, for example, in 'The
Monuments of Hiroshima' (where admittedly he says as much
himself):

The roughly estimated ones, who do not sort well
        with our common phrases,
Who are by no means eating roots of dandelion,
        or pushing up the daisies.

The more or less anonymous, to whom no human idiom
        can apply,
Who neither passed away, or on,
        nor went before, nor vanished on a sigh.

                                        (CP, 19)

During his time in Singapore, Enright became preoccupied—
perhaps harassed would be a better word—by three related
anxieties: one of a politico-moral kind, having to do with man's
own nature; one with the condition of the poet's own liberalism; and one with the function of his poetry. The Singapore

government was close to being a benevolent autarchy, run by people convinced they knew what was best for the citizens. It seemed to Enright that something was happening to the nature of man himself: 'But now we have fallen on evil times, / Ours is the age of goody-goodiness' ('To Old Cavafy, from a New Country'). The seven devils have been cast out by experts on government, psychiatry, and social engineering:

> They are planning to kill the old Adam,
> Perhaps at this moment the blade is entering.
>
> And when the old Adam has ceased to live,
> What part of us but suffers a death?
>
> The body still walks and talks,
> The mind performs its mental movements.
>
> There is no lack of younger generation
> To meet the nation's needs. Skills shall abound.
>
> They inherit all we have to offer.
> Only the dead Adam is not transmissive.
>
> (CP, 67–8)

In these circumstances the poet finds himself questioning the quality and point of his own convinced beliefs. What was it really like, that private and confident liberalism? The certainties of one's past begin to look, in the face of the brutishness and stupidity of this century, attenuated and disconsolate. Once he had his finger on 'The pulse of a large and noteworthy people' ('The Ancient Anthropologist'):

> That was long ago. Today I'm as you find me.
> All my articulations flapping freely,
> Free from every prejudice, shaking all over.
>
> (CP, 75)

'Misgiving at Dusk' comes naturally to mind at this point. It uses the nimbler leaner line Enright has now arrived at, but is also, though savagely, in touch with the sensuous tone of the earlier work. The scene is summoned in a bare couplet; in the next ten lines the intrusion of the public world clashes with the resistance of the private world; and in the last verse the poet brings in the continuance of the natural world and its ferocious operations:

In the damp unfocused dusk
Mosquitoes are gathering.

Out of a loudspeaker
Comes loud political speaking.
If I could catch the words
I could not tell the party.
If I could tell the party
I would not know the policy.
If I knew the policy
I could not see the meaning.
If I saw the meaning
I would not guess the outcome.

It is all a vituperative humming.
Night falls abruptly hereabouts.
Shaking with lust, the mosquitoes
Stiffen themselves with bloody possets.
I have become their stews.
Mist-encrusted, flowers of jasmine glimmer
On the grass, stars dismissed from office.

(CP, 71)

That follows (in *The Old Adam*) a section of poems that have
expressed anxiety and doubt as to the capacity of poetry, in poems
such as 'Silences', and 'Poet Wondering What He Is Up To', and
the bitter, less successful, 'Works Order' (in which the poet
sharply fires instructions at himself about the sort of poem he
is allowed to write). Worse still, even the patterns of nature raise
questions about the propriety or the sense of a gentle, liberal
humanism, as we see in the poem 'A Liberal Lost', which treats
this subject in a way that is at once casual and dreadful:

Seeing a lizard
Seize in his jaws
A haphazard moth,

With butcher's stance
Bashing its brainpan
Against the wall,

It was ever your rule
To race to the scene,
Usefully or not.

> (More often losing
> The lizard his meal, not
> Saving the moth.)
>
> Now no longer.
> Turning away, you say:
> 'It is the creature's nature,
>
> He needs his rations.'
> And in addition
> The sight reminds you
>
> Of that dragon
> Watching you with jaws open
> (Granted, it is his nature,
>
> He needs his rations),
> And—the thing that nettles you—
> Jeering at your liberal notions.
>   (CP, 71–2)

Enright returned to Britain, and two books of poems later, published *The Terrible Shears* (1973), a sequence about his childhood and life in the Twenties and Thirties. There are occasions in his verse when he shows a certain sincere ingeniousness in discovering a wrong, a degree too much spontaneity, almost chattiness in the telling. It is as though the poem has been plucked from the place of creation before the final formulation has evolved. There are examples of this, particularly in the autobiographical sequence, which are too personal and conscious, and in which the indignation—recollected—is sometimes too indignant. But when the creative process has come to its full term, it is hard to find fault with a work that constitutes an original species of poetic sociology, written for the most part in a constraining rhythm, at the furthest distance from song. It conveys the special quality, pinched and docile, of a certain kind of working-class life during Enright's childhood. Quite early on in the sequence, however, we have a clue to the boy Enright's exceptional response, in 'And Two Good Things' [in Infant School]:

> Listening to Miss Anthony, our lovely Miss,
> Charming us dumb with *The Wind in the Willows*.

> Dancing Sellinger's Round, and dancing and
> Dancing it, and getting it perfect forever.
>
>   (CP, 123)

These electric lines, communicating in their context with such joyous and springing rhythm the irreversible moment of imaginative discovery, lead me to try to offer at this point my own subjective specification of the main qualities of Enright's mature poetry. There is a near perfect fit of idea and form, a fit which depends on accuracy of definition. Next there is the rhythm, the life of the movement in the line is unflagging in pace and variety. There is wit which issues effortlessly into irony, together with a discursive reasoning habit of mind. And if we add that the clarity of idea, verbal precision, and springing line—Blake's 'determinate and bounding form'—express attitudes that are on the side of generosity and liberality, then we shall have the principal notes of Enright's personal tone—the accents of Enright, as it were, which are so much more appealing than 'the accents of Brecht' in the poem of that name.

The authentic accent can be seen in 'How Many Devils Can Dance on the Point . . .', from *Daughters of Earth* (1972), which begins with a potent Marlovian conclusion—if the expression is permissible:

> Why, this is hell,
> And we are in it.
> It began with mysterious punishments . . .

No shade of feeling is carried outside the precisely denotated and arctic intensity of despair. The internal logic of the poem proceeds by a series of linked and devastating judgements; the argument has the manner of a medieval disputation, which succeeds by excluding every possible conclusion but the final one:

> Except that—
> Lucid, strict and certain,
> Shining, wet and hard,
> No mystery at all.
> Why, this is hell.
>
>   (CP, 111–12)

Irony, the idiom of implication and double-talk (in the sense of duality), is pervasive in Enright in many modes and intensities.

Sometimes it is, as he has said of Chaucer in his essay on irony, *The Alluring Problem* (1988), 'delicate, recessed in its context', at others more positive and patent. It is an important influence in the two sequences, *Paradise Illustrated* and *A Faust Book*, in that an ironic tone is what makes it even possible for a humanist to avoid the ultimate act of faith otherwise required to treat the ancient theme of God and the Devil. But he can, in the wake of Marlowe and Goethe, and many others, use these concepts, or much of what has been traditionally symbolized by them. In this the poet, as in so much else, is the true representative of mankind, particularly now when we are all theoretical agnostics and practising Manichaeans. The ironic poet is simultaneously conscious of the contradictions of orthodoxy and aware of the weighty validity that the myths persistently sustain.

A Humanist Poet?

P. N. FURBANK

I SUPPOSE one of the rules of humanism, and maybe the most important one, is not leaving oneself out of the equation. It is a matter of remembering that one's listeners may feel like saying, feel like saying *derisively*, 'Listen to who's talking!' It is a very relevant gibe, potentially a profound one, and it is extraordinary how often one feels like making it. I do not think that Positivists of the Auguste Comte school, who practised the Religion of Humanity, can have been very sound humanists, for to the waggish or the evil-minded it sounds like making a religion of yourself. 'Look who's talking!'

For similar reasons it never seemed to me proper for George Steiner to ask us to admire the impressive spectacle of poets going silent. For imagine him, or oneself, as a professional critic, actually coming up to a poet and telling him or her how much one approves of their silence, even trying to turn the remark into a pretty compliment. It would be a case of forgetting who you are and whom you are talking to. The same might be said of Marx (though in fact Marx deserves to be called a 'humanist') when in 1843 he saw hope and redemption for future genera-tions in the very extremeness of dispossession, the loss of its very humanity, of the existing proletariat. For imagine a flesh-and-blood intellectual actually asking a flesh-and-blood worker to make a more than Christ-like sacrifice on behalf of posterity. It would be a most grotesque scene. There are things, and this seems to be one of them, that no one is in a position to say.

Or take Wordsworth and his 'Old Cumberland Beggar'. The poem is a plea against imprisoning this old man in a workhouse, and its arguments are these (was a more selfish set of arguments ever propounded?) The beggar makes us count our own blessings and realize how well off we are. He encourages us to perform our little acts of charity: a neighbour, though poor herself, gives the beggar a handful of meal every Friday and then,

> Returning with exhilarated heart
> Sits by the fire, and builds her hope of heaven.

Thirdly, we are to let him struggle picturesquely with cold winds and winter snows because the hope in his heart is an emotion worthy of reverence. (Presumably the hope in his heart might have something to do with finding shelter?) Fourthly, we ought to allow the old man the chance to enjoy the pleasant sights and sounds of nature—though in fact he cannot, being too deaf to hear the bird-song and too bent with rheumatics to be able to look up at the sunset.

The objection here is not quite the same, for Wordsworth seems to be clear as to whom he is talking: it is the Government, the parish authorities, and his educated readers, lovers of the picturesque—certainly not to the old man. Nevertheless, unless Wordsworth really was a hypocrite on a Chadband-like or Pecksniffian scale, something has gone wrong with his logic here. He is trying to say what no one is in a position to say.

But then, with all his virtues, Wordsworth was not a humanist, nor, essentially, much interested in people as people. To be a humanist, as to be a Wordsworth, calls for imagination, but of a rather special kind. The talent of the humanist, it seems to be emerging, is for asking 'who is saying what to whom?' and 'what are the things that can, or cannot be said, remembering that speakers are not angels nor extraterrestrial visitants but are subject to the same contractual laws of discourse as their listeners?' In our own century who, would one say, most possess this kind of imagination, anyway among Anglo-Saxon writers? The names that spring to mind are E. M. Forster, Philip Larkin, and D. J. Enright.

It must be a satisfaction to Enright to have written at least one poem that manages to say everything he most wants to say and does so supremely well. I am referring to 'Written Off', from the collection *Some Men are Brothers*. Here it is (quoted in full, since it is not included in the *Collected Poems*):

Written Off

> There is no shame in looking at him,
> If you like, if 'him' it is.
> He will not see you looking at it;
> It knows no pride that's 'his'.

Blind with bread, he won't eye your cake;
Like silk, against that skin, the rice-straw lies.
Waking, he sleeps;
And when he sleeps, he dies. And when he dies?

Hence he is harmless, for he lacks desire,
And all that might invite gods' angers or a thief.
Though brakes scream as he starts across the road,
No driver screams at such, a slow blown leaf.

The death of every taste lies here,
Mummied in barely rustling straw.
What could you make of such vast absences?
Blank mind, blank sense, blank bolted door.

Such things exist? But no, they don't.
The older poets, like the lice
Whose fathers' teeth were broken on his hide,
Soon found him fruitless. You're less nice?—

The shame would be to write of such a thing.
A little money, if you like, you may—
If you can find his hand.
That's perfectly all right. As you might pay
The entrance fee to some museum.
Not Art, though. Natural History, say.

   The poem is one of many of his about the utterly destitute, the
beggars and worse-off than beggars, of the streets of the Far East.
They are poems posing the question that a humanist has to ask
and to answer: what are the limits of humanism? It is of course
the question expressed in the title of the volume, *Some Men are
Brothers*: 'Homo sum; humani nil a me alienum puto'; they are
fine words but, as everyone knows, and a humanist especially,
they are quite false. Thus to define the point at which they become
false, and to do so with so much compunction, honesty, and
accuracy, is a great achievement on Enright's part in itself. But
it is significant that 'Written Off' is, for Enright, a more than
usually 'brilliant' poem, taut in its structure and full of the
cunningest gestures, unnerving surprises, and subtle plays on
words.
   What a powerful gesture it is, that jolting question in 'And
when he sleeps, he dies. And when he dies?' evoking Hamlet's

soliloquy only to drag us back from it to a much more agonizing puzzle—what can it mean, not just metaphysically but even semantically, for a creature dead already to 'die'? (Actually, one can imagine Philip Larkin bringing off such a stroke, in his own different manner.)

Or consider the brilliance of the very title of Enright's poem, which in its ambiguity, epitomizes its whole drift. For the poem has not one protagonist but two. The forlorn protagonist has been written off by society and by humankind, including the poet himself, the poem's other protagonist; but at the same time, he has been 'written off' by the poet in the sense of 'fed off', used as an occasion to earn money by his pen.

There is, the poem insists on it, a kind of shame attaching to such a poem, one which says 'Here is a fellow human creature with whom I can have no possible connection'; and the shame increases in proportion to the poem's literary brilliance. There is a heartlessness built into the whole business of being a professional writer. It is a truth which Wordsworth himself was aware of, though you would not guess so from his 'Old Cumberland Beggar', but for Enright it is always near the forefront of his mind. He faces it squarely in the preceding poem in the collection, the much less complex but fetching one entitled 'Changing the Subject' (another nice punning Enrightesque title). The poet, 'in exasperation', has suggested to a Japanese fellow-writer that he might find something else to write about, apart from 'the moon, and flowers, and birds, and temples, / and the bare hills of the once holy city'. Well,

> It happened my hard words chimed with a new slogan,
>   a good idea, since ruined—
> 'Humanism'. So I helped on a fashion, another like
>   mambo, French chanson, and learning Russian.

The writer takes the hint and reappears in the guise of a social-realist poet, celebrating the down-and-outs who sleep in the subway and imagining with heart-warming sentiment their brave 'comradeship' and the way their 'Broken bamboo baskets, their constant companions, watch / loyally over their sleeping masters'. He asks proudly if he has not passed the test and become 'truly humanistic', writing these poems about those

Who are indescribable. Have no wives or daughters to sell.
  Not the grain of faith that makes a beggar.
Have no words. No thing to express. No 'comrade'.
  Nothing so gratifying as a 'common fate'.

   .   .   .   .

'Are they miners from Kyushu?' Neither he nor I will
  ever dare to ask them.
For we know they are not really human, are as apt themes
  for verse as the moon and the bare hills.

(CP, 31–2)

It follows very naturally from these concerns that Enright's attitude towards writing and himself as a writer is both earnest and throwaway. He has acquired a style all right, and a very personal one. There is great originality in the form of his poems, with their gingerly, stop–start progress, moving insouciantly, even you might say bloody-mindedly, in and out of standard verse-forms. But this has not come from any Yeatsian, or even Larkinesque, passion for perfecting a style. Aestheticism, for good humanist reasons, is continually a bogy for him. He is content, with a touch of laziness, for there to be, in half his poems, a good deal of casual lunging-about, rather hit-or-miss in character, before they tighten up and deliver their knock-out punch.

Equally, this itinerant moralist does not give the impression of looking round for moral lessons; which is, perhaps, another kind of laziness, but certainly a fruitful one. For what we find instead is something more impressive: a dogged commitment to confront any moral, however humiliating, that manages to obtrude itself on him—and thousands do. By some odd law, the sheer abundance of his poems serves as a kind of proof of their genuineness, and the more he repeats himself, the more, not less, seriously are we inclined to take him.

What is a humanist poet, anyway this humanist poet, in pursuit of? It seems that we can give a rough answer. It is 'the real thing', what Forster calls 'life', what Tolstoy called 'What men live by'— the reality that too much thinking about 'realism', the human thing that too much thinking even about 'humanism', may not help us to recognize. This is the quarry of Enright, that subtle and ribald detector of phoneyness. The real thing will be nothing quite expected, it will be marginal ('marginal' would not be a bad epithet for Enright as a poet), and it will be shared or shareable.

These are all of them characteristics captured in the beautiful and mysterious poem 'Meeting an Egyptian at a Cocktail Party':

> And so he is an exile. Not for doing something,
> Just for feeling. In these dark and gentle eyes
> I see his country. And my past. And rather more.
>
> Just for feeling free he's forced to stray.
> And still how right and readily he knows
> Before I speak it what I mean. And helps me mean.
>
> Behind these dark and gentle eyes
> I watch the river flow, unangry and forever.

Feeling so strong a *rapport*, the two instinctively want to protect it:

> We wonder why we whisper—like conspirators—
>
> We do not talk of politics or gods or sex.
> Sun on the salt-lake sparkles in the darkened room,
> Rises a cloud of witness clearer than our words.

As 'Written Off' was about frontiers, so this is about margins, typographical and moral.

> A meeting, like this poem, marginal.
> You that hold back a press of blackening hate,
> Margins, keep free a space where we may meet again!
>   (from *Some Men Are Brothers*)

'Real', a word more debased and faceless than most, is one that Enright is surprisingly bold with, and never more poignantly and persuasively than in the much-quoted and well-known poem, 'The Noodle-Vendor's Flute'. It is a wonderful poem, resourceful in its form in a way that is true of only a handful of Enright's poems. Not that one feels it to be any more contrived or less spontaneous; but, in its irregular way, it seems to develop a firmer and completer shape. The regular falling rhythm of the first nine lines has some vague mimetic relationship to the noodle-vendor's monotonous tune. Time, next, for the usual Enright shying-away from set verse-forms, and the poem lapses for a while into a near-prose shuffle; then the lift into eloquence ('Yet still the pathos of that double tune . . .')—an eloquence that, though halted sometimes and undercut by mild ironies, takes over the poem, steadily growing in solemnity.

In a real city, from a real house,
At midnight by the ticking clocks,
In winter by the crackling roads:
Hearing the noodle-vendor's flute,
Two single fragile falling notes . . .
But what can this small sing-song say,
Under the noise of war?
The flute itself a counterfeit
(Siberian wind can freeze the lips),
Merely a rubber bulb and metal horn
(Hard to ride a cycle, watch for manholes
And late drunks, and play a flute together).
Just squeeze between gloved fingers,
And the note of mild hope sounds:
Release, the indrawn sigh of mild despair . . .
A poignant signal, like the cooee
Of some diffident soul locked out,
Less than appropriate to cooling macaroni.
Two wooden boxes slung across the wheel,
A rider in his middle age, trundling
This gross contraption on a dismal road,
Red eyes and nose and breathless rubber horn.
Yet still the pathos of that double tune
Defies its provenance, and can warm
The bitter night.
Sleepless, we turn and sleep.
Or sickness dwindles to some local limb.
Bought love for one long moment gives itself.
Or there a witch assures a frightened child
She bears no personal grudge.
And I, like other listeners,
See my stupid sadness as a common thing.
And being common,
Therefore something rare indeed.
The puffing vendor, surer than a trumpet,
Tells us we are not alone.
Each night that same frail midnight tune
Squeezed from a bogus flute,
Under the noise of war, after war's noise,
It mourns the fallen, every night,
It celebrates survival—
In real cities, real houses, real time.

(CP, 32)

But also, when one comes to think of it, what a perfect analogue, not to say antidote, this poem is to Wordsworth's 'Old Cumberland Beggar'! Between the situation of Wordsworth's beggar and Enright's noodle-vendor, the one struggling 'with frosty air and winter snows' and having the 'chartered wind' beat his grey locks against his withered face, and the other trundling 'cooling macaroni' by night on a pot-holed road in a Siberian wind, there is not too much to choose; but, on the other hand, the profit we are asked to obtain from them is of a very different order. In Enright's vision, the point is there is no calculation, no profit-and-loss account; the gain is entirely gratuitous, an unexpected blessing or 'plus' for which the noodle-vendor has neither to be sacrificed nor thanked. The noodle-vendor himself is to be treated neither in the Romantic nature-poet manner—that is to say, as if he were just a part of the landscape, a rock, or a picturesque wind-blown tree—nor in the utilitarian-moralist manner, in terms of social benefit—in other words, of what one can get out of him. His existence as a particular fellow human being is acknowledged fully, and in a casual and rueful way we are tempted to try it on as a symbol for our own; but on the other hand, it is not in the least invaded. It is just that, by an accident (the tune of his absurd little rubber horn) his existence has this power of invading, slipping through bedroom windows, and overcoming even the noise of war. To revert to my theory of humanist writing: the things that Enright says in this poem, and elsewhere, are the ones that he—and we in his shoes—*are* in a position to say.

The Terrible Shears:
More Notes on Nostalgia

DAVID ELLIS

POEM VIII in I. A. Richards's *Practical Criticism* offered his victims
ample opportunity for denouncing sentimentality. When a
woman's singing takes a poet 'back down the vista of years' until
he remembers sitting under the piano his mother was playing
and even 'old Sunday evenings at home with winter outside /
And hymns in the cosy parlour', it was not difficult to know what
to think. But the absence of difficulty did not mean that the
thoughts were necessarily accurate. Too many readers of 'Piano'
(Richards and others were to suggest) failed to notice that
Lawrence is fully aware that he has been betrayed into memories
of childhood in spite of himself and by the 'insidious mastery of
song'; or that his final weeping 'like a child for the past' is
accompanied in his mind by a loss of manhood. The rhythm of
the poem, it was claimed, was in any case resistant to any easy,
self-indulgent yielding to nostalgia.

A striking feature of this discussion is the degree to which all
parties take for granted that nostalgia is a bad thing. When
innocent pleasures are so thin on the ground, one might wonder
why. In the 1920s, it was still possible to appeal to science for
at least part of the answer. Nostalgia is an urge to return to a
former state and closely associated therefore with the Freudian
concept of regression. In *Beyond the Pleasure Principle*, Freud
identified with the 'death instincts' any organism's reluctance to
meet the challenge of fresh stimuli in the environment and
its corresponding inclination to retreat backwards along the
evolutionary path. Resistance to regression was thus important
for the species as well as the individual. Whether or not Lawrence
himself thought this he would certainly have shared the pre-
suppositions of 'Piano''s critics and more because of the strength
of his own nostalgic or regressive impulses than in spite of them.
Someone in whom they were weak could well have conceived
the scene in the last chapter of *Lady Chatterley's Lover* where

Sir Clifford begins to use Mrs Bolton as a surrogate mother, but hardly have written it with such savagery. Between 'Piano' and those passages there is a continual and not always successful struggle in Lawrence against the narcotic lure of his early days.

The cultural veto on nostalgia continues to prevail, but an additional problem for D. J. Enright in writing about his past is that the 1920s childhood he evokes so successfully in *The Terrible Shears* was (like Lawrence's) working-class. He is not prepared to ignore the importance of this, and in a poem towards the end of the volume protests explicitly against the notion that 'class' does not matter; but he is inevitably aware of a whole group of readers who in their general twentieth-century alertness to sentimentality are particularly quick at detecting any inclination to make a 'disadvantaged' childhood the basis for sentimental appeal. These are readers who, since the 1960s especially, have been accustomed to the idea of writers who make professional capital out of social disadvantage and exploit their working-class origins. But exploitation is often in the eyes of those beholders who are in a position to arrange most things, including language, for their own benefit. A poem which seems a temporary diversion from the main subject matter of *The Terrible Shears* can be taken as a reminder of this. ' "It's the last camel", said the straw, / "The last camel that breaks our backs" ' are its opening lines; and it ends by asking to hear no more about the camel ' "With its huge and heavy feet".'

The rules of engagement for *The Terrible Shears* are established at the start of the first poem.

> We had to keep our coal out at the back;
> They wouldn't give us a bath.

This dates a common myth to a quite specific, later phase in the development of council housing and informs those who might still be tempted to entertain it of the real conditions of working-class life in the 1920s—hardly different in the bathing department than they had been for Lawrence thirty years earlier. Characteristically wary in their humour and indirection, the lines suggest a suspicion of the outside world (in this case, the reader) which the other poems go on to show was part of the atmosphere their author grew up in. The anonymous representative of a working-class collectivity in 'They: Early Horror Film' ends by congratulating

herself on having given nothing away to the authorities who have
called at the door: ' "Yes sir, no sir, / We wouldn't know anything
about that, sir" '; and a poem which contrasts the plain-speaking
youth of today with Enright's memories of his own adolescence
begins,

> One never complained of being misunderstood!
> That in fact was what, if ruefully, one hoped for.

Experience has so often taught the forebears of these figures that
no good ever came from drawing attention to yourself, that distrust
of bosses, policemen, teachers, and clergymen is an inherited
characteristic. A more positive consequence is the *pudeur* which
develops from a healthy pride (why give oneself away to those
who in their condescending ignorance can only simulate concern or friendliness?) and which in the mature poet has been
transformed into the refined emotional reticence and talent for
scrupulous understatement that allow him to step through the
minefield of childhood memory uncompromised. In his rather
grim narrative of a postman father who died in middle-age from
lung cancer ('without benefit of smoking'), and a mother who
was then obliged to give up her council house to become a
housekeeper, there was plenty of scope for wrong directions. But
at no point in *The Terrible Shears* are readers made to feel that they
are being appealed to for sympathy or allowed to forget that this
is an ordinary destiny, no more deserving of commemoration than
any other, but no less so either.

The success is partly attributable to an unusual form. *The Prelude*
failed to establish any great vogue for autobiography in verse and
Wordsworth's poem is in any case a continuous narrative. As the
subtitle indicates, *The Terrible Shears* is made up of '*Scenes* from
a Twenties Childhood'—fleeting recollections as of (for example)
one of the 'bad things' in infant school: 'Bowing our heads to
a hurried nurse, and / Hearing the nits rattle down on the paper'.
They are snapshots from memory in an arrangement which is only
loosely and implicitly chronological. In a consecutive verse or
prose narrative of the conventional variety, where a unifying form
of address needs to be established and so much more has to be
said, it would be harder to maintain the fine hygienic balance in
relations with the reader. A poem in which Memory is compared
to a shopkeeper who studies his customers' moods and knows

what to offer them, is a warning against congratulating its author
too warmly on the selection of his material. 'Only the mad and
the dying / Have the run of the establishment', whilst the rest
of us are apt to think we are making choices when we are merely
taking what we have been given. But the credit is his for the
delicate control he exercises over the remnants which are on offer.
An illustration is the second in a series of five poems about
Christmas, 'Jingle Bells':

> Our presents were hidden on top of the cupboard.
> Climbing up, we found a musical box, in the shape
> Of a roller, which you pushed along the floor.
>
> This was for our new sister, she was only
> A few months old, her name was Valerie.
>
> Just before Christmas (this I know is a memory
> For no one ever spoke of it) the baby quietly
> Disgorged a lot of blood, and was taken away.
>
> The musical box disappeared too,
> As my sister and I noted with mixed feelings.
> We were not too old to play with it.

The first poem in this series describes bottles of Vimto squatting on
the 'knife-creased' tablecloth and has obvious class connotations:
'It is Christmas—/ Someone will pay for this.' So too does the
fourth in which Enright recalls that his father was not often
around at Christmas (a bad time for postmen). But he is dealing
here with a misfortune that affects all levels of society. Alertness
to the difficulty of treating it is apparent in the insistence that
the memory is authentic: an inescapable fact of family history.
(A subsequent glimpse, in the third poem, of his mother weeping
over the kitchen sink, 'Milk, warm and unwanted, draining
away', he is not prepared to vouch for so confidently.) The
problem is that the pain of the episode can only have been fully
felt by his parents and particularly by his mother, to whom
The Terrible Shears is dedicated. To claim too large a part of it,
retrospectively, would be false. The solution is to recall the
contemporary situation and how the healthy self-absorption of
children disposes of what for them can never be much more than
bemusement at adult grief.

The difference between how things were at the time and what they now seem preoccupies all autobiographers. In Book IV of *The Prelude*, Wordsworth imagines how, as he leans over the side of a boat to peer into his past, he is perplexed by reflections in the water of his own immediate environment. The discrepancy between then and now is problematic for those writing about their younger selves because their ambition is usually a true account; but the great fictional classics of childhood have made it more familiar to us as a reliable artistic resource. It is not hard (for example) to imagine how, in a situation analogous to 'Jingle Bells', Dickens would have used the discrepancy to generate pathos; and the opening of *Great Expectations* makes it abundantly clear that it can also be a source of comedy. The way the narrator of that novel makes affectionate fun of his young self's fears and credulity can begin to seem remorseless or patronizing on re-reading, but whoever writes about the past is always obliged to come to terms with two apparently distinct moments in time. Joyce's radical response at the beginning of *A Portrait of the Artist* may make many readers feel that this is what it is really like to be very young ('He was baby tuckoo. The moocow came down the road where Betty Byrne lived: she sold lemon platt'); but for others the mimicry of infant perception will only fill the mind with admiration for the grown-up's virtuosity. It will also only confirm that, strictly speaking, there is in autobiography never more than the one moment of writing since, however completely authors succeed in re-entering their childhood world, they do so fully equipped with adult powers of expression. Yet there are recognizably different levels of intensity at which autobiographers or novelists 'relive' earlier days: gifts of more or less vivid recall. The peculiar vividness of Lawrence's is evident in early poems like 'Piano' or indeed in *Sons and Lovers* where the distinction between fiction and autobiography does not have to be insisted on so strictly. What it produces there is the paradox that the author who from the beginning of his career was familiar with the great nineteenth-century denunciations of industrial society, and was later to be responsible for several memorable examples himself (in *Women in Love* or *Lady Chatterley's Lover*), tends to give the impression that the industrial Midlands were as good a place as any to grow up in. This is partly because much of Part One of *Sons and Lovers* is seen through the eyes of Paul and the resentments of children rarely stray far beyond their immediate circle. The intensity of their self-absorption not only means they can take the death of siblings in their stride but also that they are unlikely to relate their day-to-day misfortunes to a wider social context, even supposing they had conceptual power. Feeling his life in every limb, as Wordsworth says of the little girl in 'We are Seven', the young Paul Morel is free of the nagging and permanent causes of dissatisfaction which affect older people, and the impression retained of his childhood is that it is essentially happy, despite the several objective social reasons the reader is given for thinking it miserable. Like Wordsworth, Lawrence can appear to repossess entirely the early childhood world of constantly renewable animal spirit and mercifully limited horizons. There is an implicit tribute to the unusual power they both possess when at one moment in *The Terrible Shears* Enright insists that his own childhood was not a constant succession of disasters,

> The happiness you must take as read,
> The writing of it is so difficult.

If happiness is relatively absent from Enright's record of his childhood, there is none the less a certain amount of contentment.

> Threepence on Saturday afternoons,
> A bench along the side of the hall—
> We looked like Egyptian paintings,
> But less composed.
>
> Sometimes a film that frightened us
> And returned at nights.
> Once *Noah's Ark*, an early talkie
> We took for non-fiction.
>
> Cheapest was the home kino.
> Lying in bed, you pressed on your eyes,
> Strange happenings ensued.
>
> But the story was hard to follow
> And your eyeballs might fall in.
> Fatigued, you fell asleep.
>
> ('The Pictures')

In the first stanza the poet visualizes his former self and in the second he takes the opportunity of correcting a former error. But thereafter, and especially with the reported folklore of the eyeballs falling in, he is drawn wholly back into former days. In 'Jingle Bells' this pattern precludes any suspicion of an appeal for sympathy; here it discourages any form of social comment. What is narrow and constricted in any childhood can only be perceived by comparison, and the child's world is one of powerful self-sufficiency. Its appeal might charm the reader into regretting the good old days, when children had to amuse themselves, but that danger is counteracted five poems later in '1,000 Useful Things To Do About the House'. There Enright remembers how he and his sister made 'several miles of cork-wool' and 'Enough / Papier-mâché bowls to stock the V & A' . . .

> Now people sit and watch television.
> Which is often quite instructive—
> You can even listen to talks about the
> Conspicuous creativity of the old days.

So much for nostalgia of the political variety. The irony is far broader here than is usual in *The Terrible Shears*, but there is room for it because it is not required to coexist with any evocation of childhood absorption in even such activities as the manufacture of cork-wool.

Sons and Lovers suggests that the relative absence of 'happiness' from *The Terrible Shears*—either of specific joyful occasions or a more pervasive exhilaration—ought to mean that it functions more directly as social criticism. But where the child's view predominates, as it eventually does in both 'Jingle Bells' and 'The Pictures', any form of social commentary must be incidental. For those with high, self-regulating standards of emotional decency, to complain of hardships not perceived as such at the time is an even trickier matter than protesting against conditions of life which, as an escapee from a certain class, the complainant no longer has to endure. The consequence is that 'background' can seem on occasion a matter of relative, if not complete, indifference.

> The canal was nearby, the cut we called it.
> A sullen water, it refused to bear away
> What we had given it. It gave us back dead eels.
> All the sickness of the town lay there.
> As I grew up, I came to hate all water.

Over our garden wall the railway embankment
Rose steeply. In summer the grass caught fire.
At an upstairs window, with Granma,
I watched the flames, pale and fierce and quick.
Fire was my favourite element.

('Fire and Water'*)

Pater claimed that Wordsworth would have been very much the same poet had he been born in Surrey, and there are no doubt ways in which it doesn't much matter whether one is brought up in the back streets of some industrial town or the garden suburbs. This poem recalls both an Elizabethan method for analysing the grounds of personality (is it the flames themselves which are 'pale and fierce and quick' or their observer?), and the more recent speculations of Gaston Bachelard. Yet even our contact with the elements is rarely unmediated by social circumstances and apparently 'primary' affinities and revulsions have more often than not a social context. It is not from a canal that everyone forms their first impressions of water. In 'A Difference', Enright points out how you would have had to loathe yourself to drown yourself in the cut—'A person with any self-respect / Made use of the river'; and 'Shades of the Prison House' describes fear of the workhouse as being 'like a black canal / Running through our lives'. It is to the workhouse that the Granma has to be sent when Enright's father dies and his mother is obliged to keep house for a 'troublesome old man'. This episode is described in 'Geriatrics'—one of the longest poems in *The Terrible Shears*. Distress and guilt (Granma 'defended me, her I failed to defend') make it a crucial moment in the growth of the poet's mind not least because, as the following poem—'Early Therapy'—explains, 'It started me writing poems'. But it can also be seen as the incident which imposed an initial political stance: 'Perhaps it had to be done, / Did it have to be done like that?'

There is not much sign in *The Terrible Shears* of subsequent deviation from this attitude. When the abilities of which the poetry-writing was one indication took Enright to Cambridge, he found that the social ills he had come to know had been correctly diagnosed but that the solutions proposed left him sceptical:

* Omitted by author from *Collected Poems*.

'. . . I wasn't too sure of the cure. / And couldn't quite believe / Things had once been so much better.' Working-class suspicion of authority extends to those with proposals for leading the disadvantaged into better times. The inherited lesson of experience here is that, although the proposers themselves might benefit from change, those who are persuaded to follow will be left very much as they were before. ('It's the same the whole world over', as the song says). Social life is dominated by large-scale necessities which, as in the case of Granma, can only be alleviated by minor interventions on the individual level. Enright is both a sharer and critic of this conservatism. Anger at the idea that class is unimportant is provoked by the memory of a woman who told him, '(With a loudness I supposed was upper-class)', that Cambridge was not for the likes of him: 'Her sentiments were precisely those of the / Working class. Unanimity on basic questions / Accounts for why we never had the revolution'. This perception is an additional reason why he is not inclined to sentimentalize his origins or in any danger of being asked, like Paul Morel, how it is that if he so admires the warmth of the common people he doesn't consort with his father's friends. A 'Sentimental Journey' takes him back to the street where he was born only to find himself eyed suspiciously by Asians who feel he might have come to collect the payments on their cars. This is the third poem from the end of *The Terrible Shears*. The last two continue to illustrate the complications of his attitude. In the first, Enright confesses that although he has been accustomed to dropping into bars all over the world, he is still frightened by the ladies of Leamington who take their refreshment in 'the Cadena on Victoria Parade'. Still intimidating, they must be still unforgiven. The final poem recalls a schoolgirl who lost a leg when she was knocked down by a bus but then went on to become a local celebrity as, making light of her disability, she did well at school and later married.

> That means it wasn't a bad life.
> No one was dragged out of bed by
> Armed men. Children weren't speared
> Or their brains dashed out. I don't
> Remember seeing a man starve to death.
>
> That's something we shouldn't forget—
> That we don't remember things like that.

The poem is called 'Large Mercies'. Life, it suggests, could have been much worse and, as subsequent travel has given the author the opportunity to establish, usually is for most people. In which case, poets might as well confine themselves to the traditional concern with relationships between individuals. That at least will mean that they will still have something to do after the revolution which 'unanimity on basic questions' has up till now delayed. The balance of scepticism in *The Terrible Shears* inclines towards the idea that they would then in fact have even more to do.

Enright would have arrived in Cambridge about ten years too late to give his views on 'Piano', but that is not a poem which could have stayed in his mind as a model when he came to write about his own childhood. Saved or not by its self-consciousness, it is too obviously 'poetic' in manner and diction. More relevant would have been some of the poems Lawrence had turned to writing by the time *Practical Criticism* was published, a 'pansy' like 'The Mosquito Knows' for example: 'The mosquito knows full well, small as he is / he's a beast of prey. / But after all / he only takes his bellyful, / he doesn't put my blood in the bank.' Yet even *Pansies* are in general more lyrical, less resolutely bare, than the poems in *The Terrible Shears*, which are an extreme example of what one could call linguistic puritanism, if it were easy to associate puritans with humour. The ordinariness of their language is a tribute to, but not a reflection of, the world they describe since that, like most other worlds, chugs along on cliché. Some familiarity with the clichés concerned—local knowledge—is required to appreciate how deftly they are both evoked and avoided, and so much depends in these poems on hearing a particular tone of voice that it is hard to imagine how they could be translated. Their rigorous laconic manner is a protection against sentimental regret or the excitements of class prejudice, but the lack of adornment means that the features which distinguish them from flat statement are necessarily subtle and unobtrusive. Wordsworth set out to write the *Lyrical Ballads* in a common language which was nevertheless 'selected' and purified from 'its real defects, from all lasting and rational causes of dislike or disgust'. It was a programme whose qualifications made it easy to ridicule, but the best way he could discover to express solidarity with ordinary life whilst avoiding the hypocrisy of pretending he belonged to it. The common speech of *The Terrible Shears* is a similarly ideal idiom because it involves using common words with uncommon distinction: inhabiting a world of ordinary language in a peculiarly individual way. One cannot imagine Enright being too distressed by those for whom this is not obvious. Although it is unlikely he still has the same hopes of being misunderstood he harboured as a boy, to be perceived as ordinary and have his poetic credentials ignored would be a temporary alleviation of the anomaly of his situation. The 'Acknowledgements' at the end of *The Terrible Shears* begin with a reference by Richard Hoggart to the scholarship boy: 'But he has been equipped for hurdle-jumping; so he merely dreams of getting on, but somehow not in the world's way.' The poems it follows convey more interestingly and precisely why it might seem less important to be confused with the crowd than run even the slightest risk of pretentious singularity.

'The Facts of Life'
(on reading D. J. Enright's
The Terrible Shears)

PATRICIA BEER

Rudimentary as light, the facts of life tumble
Down on to a world of trees, each one unique,
Each one a filter, through which a story wriggles.
Over the floor of the forest these stories,
These confessions, stretch out in bright hieroglyphs.

Some of the facts get caught up in the boughs
And itch till doomsday. Some flutter vividly
And fall to the ground like confetti, single moments
Of a ceremony. The more uneasy the tree
The more eloquent the pattern it composes.

Poets' minds make the best filters; they deal in fragments.
Their villains never get through the sieve whole.
Even Pontius Pilate and Judas would land piecemeal.
In this book the ungrateful officer Crawford
Arrives as a bite-sized anecdote about biscuits.

In it, too, death has no context. Men fall dead
Off bridges and at railway stations with no word
Of afterwards or before. The disappearance
Of a baby oozes in drops of undrunk milk.
That is childhood, grief in the middle of nothing.

Facts come through the leaves with no judgement of their own.
Like light they kill or cure regardless. They are selected.
They are rejected too and the veto is absolute.
In one golden patch the shadow of a terrible leaf
Has raised its hand and spread its fingers to say 'Halt'.

Shadow Play
D. J. Enright's Books for Children

NAOMI LEWIS

THE briefing I am given is to consider D. J. Enright as a writer of children's books. Questions at once rise up: Does he . . .? Is it . . .? Do we accept that the genre exists? Yes, it exists and it flourishes, but its frontier lines are not quite constant. Both Enid Blyton and Roald Dahl know that they are aiming specifically at the young. Yet not all works found today on the junior shelves were intended for junior readers. *Black Beauty*, that terrible indictment of human cruelty, *Uncle Tom's Cabin*, *Crusoe*, *Gulliver* (sharpest of satires), even *The Scarlet Pimpernel*, were written for adults. Still, these have not only imperishable elements of story— but the one-time codes and taboos, that still hold for younger school-age fiction.

Nor is it enough to give the lead-place to the young. *What Maisie Knew*, *The Go-Between* (most, indeed, of James and of Hartley), *A High Wind in Jamaica*—to say nothing of much contemporary fiction—are by no means children's fare. Enright's three novels— *The Joke Shop*, *Wild Ghost Chase*, and *Beyond Land's End*—all appearing in quick succession at the end of the 1970s, *are* about children, in child-situations of the fantastical sort. All are meant for the young. Whatever the motive for writing them, the choice of fantasy has plenty of precedent in adult writers trying their hand at the genre. Look back a hundred years or so for some major instances. In the 1850s, '60s, and '70s, by one of those neat arrangements of history, a number of leading adult authors—novelists, poets, philosophers, critics, theologians, mathematicians—suddenly turned to the field of children's fantasy: Ruskin, with *The King of the Golden River*; Thackerary, *The Rose and the Ring*; Kingsley, *The Water Babies*; Carroll, the Alice books; Ingelow, *Mopsa the Fairy*; MacDonald (whose many adult novels are now forgotten), *At the Back of the North Wind*, *The Princess and the Goblin*, and more. What these magnificent works exemplify is the authors' mental transference into the supernatural.

Fantasy has its own strict laws (the wish can never be greater than the wisher); yet it overrides certain difficulties, and its ranges and freedoms are vast. On his own scale, Enright, who owes not a little to these master-hands, shares with them the wild freedom granted by fantasy, as well as the sense, however illusory, of personal disguise.

Since his three child-novels are sufficiently out of print to be collectors' pieces, an account of each should be useful. In *The Joke Shop* (1976), three literate children, Robert, Jane, and Timmy ('a small boy with a large appetite for knowledge and other things'), with time on their hands and a need to keep out of their irate father's way (he's a writer of children's books), join a curious adult trio engaged in a search for a pair of lost (maybe long-lost) twins, Lily and Leslie Lacey. (These names are not the only echo of Carroll.) The adults are Herr Brush, a kindly man with pointed ears, a Police-Inspector Barlow, and a Mr Spock, half-mortal, half-Vulcanite; his early years were passed on the planet Vulcan and he still has 'a touch of the starbrush'. Passing the sinister Joke Shop, the children see through its dusty window what might be two other children, beckoning, and they enter: 'We were waving to warn you to go away', say the pallid twins. 'They made us stand here.' But it's too late. A door at the back of the shop opens into something like a midnight wood, and they are trapped in Shadow Land, a faint and colourless place, where light and dark work exactly in reverse.

They are lodged in a castle (the 'Shadeau') where they learn history (the Endarkenment), about John Nox (who perfected the rituals of the Black Mass), and 'the brilliant but possibly unstable philosopher Nightshade'. They are offered a choice of games (ombre; shadow boxing), their lessens (as in Carroll) making them daily (or rather, nightly) more and more shadowy. Meanwhile, in the human world, where a shadow month is scarcely an hour, they are sought by the philosophic three. The eventual flight and escape (through the back of the shop) is narrative proper, an earned reward for every diligent reader who has battled through the verbal saltimbanqueries.

Wild Ghost Chase (1978) is openly comedy. Yet it is a much more disturbing book. It has the same children and the same adult trio, now with a distinctly Chestertonian air — 'The true identities of the three were known to very few. Sometimes they had difficulty in remembering them themselves.' Spock, who admits to changing his pseudonym frequently (perhaps with reason) has now become Mock. All are involved in the problems of two misfits. One is Undine ('the adopted daughter of a Hull trawlerman and his wife'), described as a 'slender young lady, who wore a loose frock, green in colour and old-fashioned in style. Her face was pale and oval, her hair long and golden.' A phenomenal swimmer, she is obliged to hide this skill in her job at the public baths. Her trouble? She lacks a soul. The other misfit is Primula, a mild vegetarian vampire, who *has* a soul and desires to be free of its problems. 'What is a soul?' muses Enright, in the guise of one of his characters: 'A small blue thing that runs about within us?' Barlow, Brush, and Mock sense evil—the vampire Fistula, maybe, who has designs on the children, Jane especially. And in a spirited scene—the pun is unintentional— they exorcize the crazy ghost of an old television set, forever crying out its commercial wares, by playing the Great Mass for the Dead by Berlioz. Such jinks as these make the soul-crossing climax almost tame. Fancies, word-plays, disputations abound. But, as story, the parts fail to make a whole.

The third and final book, *Beyond Land's End* (1979), is probably in terms of the genre itself, the most confident and successful of the three. The children now go to Cornwall in the comfortable charge of Mr and Mrs Inspector Barlow. Also stepping westward are, of course, Brush and Mock, in response to a call from their friends in Atlantis. That fabled isle (as Mock informs us) has survived over the centuries in a great sealed air-bubble, floating just above the deep sea bed. Its kindly, peaceable people, advanced in technology of every kind, but living simply for preference, are in trouble. Some hostile Thing has found entrance and has stolen or shifted the *gravity*. 'As the western side of Atlantis sinks, so the eastern will rise. And smash into the south-west region of England. . . . Conceivably, the British Isles will be sucked wholesale beneath the waves.' A highly individual computer hints that children may be effective in countering the Evil, and there they are, welcomed into this odd, agreeable place. That computer, a sort of vulgar Oracle (and quite the most interesting character in the book), delivers throughout a stream of enigmatic, saucy, highly-charged utterances: familiar verses slightly wrong, warnings, clues, the final answer too. Following its

weird advice, Robert sets off alone at dawn and reaches, after
some hard journeying, the tunnel where the original end was
sealed. The story is solved by a Sword-in-the-Stone situation. The
soft choice of pseudo-Arthur may not please all readers. The
youngest all too often get the handsome roles. Yes, there *is* a
streak of the sentimental in Enright's writing for children. Girl
readers especially may cringe at the Wendyish Jane, so soppy over
babies. Still, Robert's heroic journey is the real stuff of story: no
need for word tricks, you will notice.

All works of fiction for the young, if you look closely, fall into
one or other of two main kinds: the concealed moral-didactic, and
the conspiratorial-subversive: 'I'm on your side against the
tiresome grown-ups.' These things have nothing to do with
readability. *The Secret Garden*, perhaps the most popular children's
book ever written, is of the first kind. So are the Narnia stories—
maybe even *Charlotte's Web*. The William books are of the second
kind. So is *Tom Sawyer*, and anything by Dahl. Nesbit has a touch
of both. Enright desires, I fancy, to be with the second lot. Boring
parents are well disposed of; the three main adults, vaguely
magical, are scarcely of a conventional kind. But he cannot resist
ideas and words, wry thoughts about the nature of life and such.
He is not as outrageously self-indulgent as Kingsley, who, (in the
manner of Rabelais) filled *The Water Babies* with lists of his hates
and loves and other informing data. Most of today's pretty
editions firmly cut them out, but they are better left in. Their
pugnacious flavour is intrinsic to the book. Enright's musings are
different. They carry a grain of doubt, of melancholy, that has
no place in the genre. That quirky business of the soul in *Wild
Ghost Chase* does have possibilities. What is gained or lost by its
presence? Its absence? He does some diverting clowning with his
source, Andersen's *The Little Mermaid*, that powerful, flawed, and
vexing tale whose theology, that assigns a 'soul' to the most
worthless of humans, but denies it to all other sentient creatures,
is the reasoning behind the vivisection laboratories and many
other evils. But he lets the idea slip away. Wilde, an admirer and
disciple of Andersen, did better. No one has matched his
audacious reversal of the old dogma in his dazzling tale, 'The
Fisherman and his Soul'.

Enright's three books have no lack of ingredients that should
make them highly edible to the book-devouring child. Have we

encountered some of them elsewhere? This hardly matters. To
be sure, the magic shop does have an echo in Wells. Shadow
Land, quite apart from the word-tricks, *is* a kind of Looking-Glass
country. A door in a cupboard opening on to a midnight forest
may well recall C. S. Lewis. Much of the detail of Shadow Land
is pure Enright, yet the Lost Boys (two of them girls) can also
be glimpsed within. Ghosts, vampires, and flying horses are free
to every fairy-tale teller. So is Atlantis, for ever lost, found, lost
like the Grail itself. Books, after all, grow out of books as trees
grow out of trees.

No—any failure in Enright's children's tales can be tracked
down to the simple matter of belief, or unbelief. You need not
be a first-rate writer to hold your readers; you must believe in
your own inventions while you are setting them down. Some
things work in Enright, some things don't, and that is the
problem. He chiefly writes from his head, and not from any
obstinate streak of childhood persistent in himself. The single
impression that stays from these books is of the teller, with his
wry, melancholy smile and sideways glance, sad clown and joker,
troubled by trouble, but not sure how to mend it, not as tough
as his own child characters.

Poetry is another matter. Enright is here on home ground, in his
own element. Again the question: is there such a thing as
children's poetry? The answer is uncertain. Some of the best-
known nursery rhymes are rags of dark adult street songs ('Ring
o' roses', 'Pop goes the weasel'). De la Mare's first book, *Songs
of Childhood*—it is one of his best—wasn't aimed at children at
all. (Nor, by the way, were Milne's verses in *When We Were Very
Young*.) Christina Rossetti's adult poems are in most child-
anthologies. Her weakest verses were written 'down' for the little
ones. On the other hand, Charles Causley's child-angled poems
are almost always good for adult reading. Well, a good poem is
a good poem. Where, then, is Enright? His voice remains so much
the same in all that he writes that there is no absolute answer.
Many of the twenty-seven poems in *Rhyme Times Rhyme* (published
in 1974 in a children's series) could appear in his adult gathering;
possibly some of them do. Certainly he writes enjoyably
about teddy bears, cats, a fat guru ('I don't care for money /
I can live for free / You call me *Holiness* / I call thee *thee*.')

'The Big Three' is a good child-poem, so is 'The Glass Ghost',
so strange, absurd, and elegant that I will quote it in full:

> One night in Japan, the typhoon was on us,
> I came home by the last train to run.
> The great wind raged this way and that,
> And the thick rain followed it.
>
> As I neared a call-box by the station,
> Its tall glass door shook free and
> Came towards me in the storm.
> Tottering from one foot to the other,
>
> We met, a ghostly man and a ghost of glass.
> Like two who meet on the street,
> And both step aside and apologize,
> Both step to the other side and apologize.
>
> The door hopped this way, then that way,
> I dodged that way, then this way.
> 'After you,' I said. The ghost was Japanese.
> '*Dōzo*,' I cried politely in the loud typhoon.
>
> I thought: if it falls on me, it will surely
> Cut my face to ribbons and slit my throat . . .
> It thought: if he falls on me, his wooden head
> Will surely shatter me to smithereens . . .
>
> Well, I am here to tell the story.
> For the wind came up behind the door
> And flung it to the ground. I jumped aside.
> Crash! And there was nothing there—
>
> Nothing in the storm, but slats of wood
> And broken glass. The ghost was laid.

Always accessible, engagingly light, his poems are not as simple
as they may seem. He scarcely changes his tone, you think, when
his mood is serious; but 'Appearances' (about a rickshaw puller),
and 'Night School in the Black Country' don't leave you after
a reading.

I Rather Like the
Sound of Foreign Languages
like Ezra Pound

PETER PORTER

STANZA six of the first part of W. H. Auden's *Letter to Lord Byron*, composed not in full ottava rima but in rhyme royal, and the chief glory of *Letters from Iceland*, the Thirties' travel book he and Louis MacNeice collaborated on, goes as follows:

> The fact is, I'm in Iceland all alone
>   —MacKenzie's prints are not unlike the scene—
> Ich hab' zu Haus, ein Gra, ein Gramophone.
>   Les gosses anglais aiment beaucoup les machines.
>   το καλον. glubit. che . . . what this may mean
> I do not know, but rather like the sound
> Of foreign languages like Ezra Pound.

When I first read these lines, more than forty years ago, I responded with an impulse I have never seriously called in question since. This ran: not that poetry is sound as such, but that poetry is mystery. Two observations should be added to Auden's remark and then I'm properly equipped to develop an arcane argument about the relativism of poetic effect and the sad lack of Pentecostal unity in our world of letters. First, a pronouncement of Robert Frost's which is now almost a cliché: 'Poetry is what gets lost in translation.' Then a somewhat less than aphoristic insight of my own derived from the principle of electricity: poetry is the incandescence produced by driving thought through the accumulated resistance of language.

Once in Yugoslavia I found myself apologizing to a local poet for the unpoetical sound of the English language. My apology was really a boast in disguise. What made English poetry great, I hinted, was the hard fighting the poet had to do to produce the final afflatus. We could leave to the Italians the easy triumphs of their musical tongue, where asking the way to the lavatory sounds like a line out of Leopardi. With us, and this would include Shakespeare, poetry is the more magnificent for being forced out of a hard-edged language offering few hostages to beauty of sound and a public demeanour more suited to the composition of mail-order catalogues than to moonlight serenades, but, at the same time, enjoying matchless flexibility of grammar and syntax. Having to earn our great effects, we ended up with finer achievements than our fellow-Europeans. My Yugoslav friend countered immediately by saying that he found English the most sheerly beautiful of all languages. It was bliss to him just to listen to the procession of sounds in an English sentence. At a public reading before this conversation in Belgrade I had heard one of my own knottier poems ('The Old Enemy', first published by D. J. Enright in *Encounter*, full of spiky words and proper nouns) read out in Serbo-Croat and had rejoiced at the solemn authority and sensual onomatopoeia of the result.

Does sound therefore attract us when it is in a foreign language and arrives relatively unburdened by the responsibility of meaning, or is it that our minds are seeking that oracular sense which poetry must once have had for its devotees? Oracles are notorious for issuing ambiguous or curdled messages. This would seem to be not just because an oracle prefers to avoid plain statement for fear of being proved wrong by events, but also because every mystery needs its hocus-pocus, its jumble of masonic tones which suggests comfort to an initiate and power to an outsider. It's important, then, to get one notorious theory about sound out of the way—I mean the Sitwellian notion that it is the sound of a poem which moves us, and not its meaning. We are speaking here of verse in our own language, where not even the most rapt concentration on vowels, consonants, plosives, alliteration, sequences of stress, etc. can obliterate syntax and meaning in a passage. The 'musical' effect of any poem owes as much to the aptness of its choice of words to bring out its meaning as it does to the mellifluousness of the words' intonation.

Generally, poets who emphasize the paramountcy of sound overdo their effects. Few can read Swinburne at his most emollient or Sitwell drenching her poems in greens, golds, jewelled and lion-tinged shades without feeling queasy. Nor is Tennyson's fabled ear at its best in lines like 'The moan of doves

in immemorial elms / And murmurings of innumerable bees.'
The real Tennysonian music (and it is uncompromisingly honey-
rich) does not need mechanical mnemonic aids: 'A land of
streams! some, like a downward smoke, / Slow-dropping veils
of thinnest lawn, did go.' Where sound comes into its own,
if not independent of meaning, then at least tangential to it,
is in nonsense poetry, especially in Edward Lear and Lewis
Carroll, and, more recently, in the verses which James Fenton
writes under the rubric 'The Empire of the Senseless'. Lear's
'The Owl and the Pussycat' is a Tennysonian lyric of the
ripest lyricism sung in a Victorian nursery by an eccentric tutor
to dispel his charges' melancholia. Lewis Carroll employs Isaac
Watts's strict metrical (i.e. musical) devices to upset the logical
morality they were employed originally by their Puritan inventor
to reinforce. It is a well-tried technique in English poetry
to use sound subversively. Sometimes this is done unconsciously,
so that Milton, for one, frequently sets verbal sensuality against
the direction of his argument. It is in his sound that Milton
especially proves Blake's comment that he was of the Devil's
party without knowing it. Though in real music, it is God
who gets the best tunes (our composers are a veritable Salvation
Army in this respect), in literature the Devil sings more
sweetly.

The previous passage was a sort of digression, since I am
concerned with the effect of the sound of foreign languages on
the English-speaking listener or reader—primarily, of course, the
listener. There are reasons for asserting that English-speakers are
notably prone to this sort of creative misunderstanding. There
is a splendid irony in the history of English as a language. In
Tudor and Jacobean times, when England was not a world force
in politics, our language was already building up its greatest
artistic achievement. Educated Englishmen travelled in Europe,
particularly in France and Italy (John Donne being exceptional
in going also to Germany), and it is reasonable to assume that
they were not as monoglot as they are today. But the frequency
of translation in these times—Florio's Montaigne, Urquhart's
Rabelais, and Harrington's Ariosto—suggests that the market for
European masterpieces was for versions of them in the native
tongue. Shakespeare was patronized by the polymath Jonson for
having 'small Latin and less Greek'. Yet the incidence of foreign

places and persons in his plays is overwhelming, as indeed it was bound to be since he, as a good box-office student, knew that Italy, the Mediterranean, and the Ancient World would bring the audiences in. His works abound in the sort of wry appreciation of exotic sound imperfectly understood which Auden points to in his stanza from *Letter to Lord Byron*. The banter in *Love's Labour's Lost* is not just a satire on pedantry; it reflects the excitement of an imperfectly educated mind playing about with the wonderful toys of language. 'They have been at a great feast of languages, and stolen the scraps' — and this applies to Shakespeare as much as to Holofernes and the rest. Our modern texts correct many of Shakespeare's quotations, whether from Classical or Renaissance Latin. I recall some modern dullard reviewing an Angus Wilson novel and remarking that Wilson was keeping up an old English tradition, already established by Shakespeare in *Henry V*, of perpetrating howlers when quoting from French. When I wrote 'imperfectly educated' above, I did not imply any slur. There is a special joy in the Pentecostal confidence of Shakespeare's use of the whole apparatus of European culture. He was not, of course, ignorant of the general field of European art and thought, he was simply a licensee of it, and not a scholar or critical commentator. How he would have got on in Padua and Mantua if he had gone there, as Henry Reed imagined his doing in his radio play, *The Great Desire I Had*, is impossible to guess.

Bernard Shaw used to assert that if a man were a master of one tongue, he would be unlikely to truly master another. The assumption seems to be that an interpreter is at the farthest remove from a poet. This carried too far is just an excuse for laziness, but as an insight into the workings of the poetic mind, it has real value. The mind of the poet is a storehouse with a very peculiar system of inventoring. What is needed for poetry is speed of connection. All poetry, and particularly dramatic poetry, must be written headlong. The stimulus to the development of the verse may be adjacence of sound or harmonic empathy as readily as some line of argument. No poem should be written with a textbook at the poet's elbow: the permissible contents must already lodge in the poet's mind. The Nine Muses are the daughters of Zeus (Creativity) by the goddess Mnemosyne (Memory). If you can't remember it, you shouldn't use it. When Pound had a library full of books to hand, his writing (the sixty

or so *Cantos* up to the middle of the war) were not just
stuffed with arcane facts but were also pernicious and cranky.
When he wrote the *Pisan Cantos*, imprisoned in a cage on
the Ligurian gulf, he was separated from his books and had to
rely on his memory. Thus early days with the Dolmetches and
others came flooding back, and he wrote the most moving of
his later poems. Shakespeare, working against the clock for
his theatre company, could pump out the bilges of his mind
and offer up some splendidly coloured stranded fish to his
audience. Sounds, like those which Caliban told Stephano and
Trinculo filled his island, were always in Shakespeare's head. He
wrote in an English richer than any before or since, and part of
his richness was a wide alluvial deposit of European language,
from Latin and Greek to Italian, French, and Celtic. James Joyce,
Shakespeare's only rival for width of reference, was not in fact
helped by knowing several languages properly. The fascination
of sound and sense in turmoil was damped down in him by
responsible acquaintance with usage and meaning. His employ-
ment of puns, for instance, is daunting and programmatic, unlike
Shakespeare's, which is playful and glancing. Shakespeare's
work is a representation of chaos which paradoxically recreates
existence by listening, shuffling, and then reorganizing God's
world for him.

As I hinted earlier on, educated Englishmen of the sixteenth
and seventeenth centuries were at home abroad (if I may put it
this way). Milton and Dr Johnson were good enough at Latin to
treat it as a living and not a dead language, and to converse more
happily in it to their hosts than in either Italian or French, though
their acquaintance with modern European languages was wider
than that of all but the greatest specialists today. The tremendous
difference between then and now lies in the global triumph of
the English language. It is English and not Latin or French which
is the twentieth century's *lingua franca*. This both bestows on
native English speakers a unique privilege in their being largely
understood everywhere, and condemns them to a notorious
indifference to foreign tongues which makes them easy prey to
the lure of the exotic. There is a further twist of the knife for those
who live in the British zone of English. That people ranging across
a spectrum from Cairo taxi-drivers to Beijing students understand

English and use it as a universal language is due to the power and authority of the United States of America. Despite the far-flung reaches of the British Empire and the less expansive domains of the Commonwealth, it is not the Children of Albion, the British Raj or the white immigrants to the Dominions who have maintained English, but Hollywood movie-makers, Broadway and Tin Pan Alley songsmiths, and Ford and Coca-Cola salesmen. Nestling with America's commercial imperialism comes America's academic predominance and the universality of the American spoken idiom.

Not to understand what you hear but yet to be fascinated by it is, I admit, almost a definition of the exotic, that false lure of literature. And here I am, contributing an essay to a book on the work of a man who has done more than most to warn us against the charm of foreign languages judged purely as sound. Dennis Enright has been an upholder of the need for sense and communication in poetry and a steady foe of obscurity, pretension, and all Cimmerian mystery, as his introduction and his selection of poems for *The Oxford Book of Contemporary Verse* shows. He also lived for the greater part of his adult working life in countries usually described in the travel brochures as 'exotic', teaching and professing English Literature to people whose grasp of our tongue ranged from the fully idiomatic to the scarcely perceptible. Thus he had every opportunity to know how irresponsible the pursuit of attractive sound for its own sake can be—the charming grace-notes of the state police! I chose to write about the exoticism of other literatures in this book partly perversely, since I wanted to explain how a provincial English-speaker like myself, whose command of both the classical and the modern world of letters is fearfully imperfect, nevertheless might be inspired to seek an empathy with the romantic, and might transgress Enright's rules (those of Kipling's 'man-on-the-spot') the better to enfranchise his own imagination. Two Enright texts give me pause—both written when he was teaching abroad. Firstly, an early poem, from *The Laughing Hyena*, entitled 'Life and Letters'. The passage is quoted from the end: Enright has been tempted by melancholy reflections on his own feelings and the mixture of sights around him to seek an easy transcendence. He firmly puts the temptation aside:

Which is why I try to write lucidly, that even I
Can understand it—and mildly, being loath to face the
                    fashionable terrors,
Or venture among sinister symbols, under ruin's shadow.
Once having known, at an utter loss, that utter
                    incomprehension
—Unseen, unsmelt, the bold bat, the cloud of jasmine,
Truly out of one's senses—it is unthinkable
To drink horror from ink, to sink into the darkness of words,
Words one has chosen oneself. Poems, at least,
Ought not to be phantoms.

                                        (CP, 14)

Who, looking at one's own all-too-easily assembled poems, could avoid the blast of that accusation—'To drink horror from ink, to sink into the darkness of words?' One's *mea culpa* should be heartfelt. And yet, says the cheeky part of the mind, words are only words. Though we may wallow in them irresponsibly yet we may also use their greater experience to amplify our own instinctive understanding. There may be a resistance movement in words (a welcoming of rhetorical or aesthetic over-reaching) which wants the inexperienced poet to don a cloak of authority he is not entitled to. In short, to let it rip, à la Rimbaud, Stevens, Ashbery. Auden comes to one's aid again:

> For poets are not celibate divines,
> Had Dante said so, who would read his lines?

I cannot believe that Enright is on the side of the magistrate's court, nor even that Leavisite responsibility makes him eschew exaggeration. What he hates is that preening of the feathers which is a stock-in-trade of the *'poète maudit'*. His own refusal to pile on the fuel may nevertheless be seen as too flattering to poetry, in quite another way. Auden's 'poetry makes nothing happen' might prove more a daunting saying to the socially responsible poet than to the lurid bard. Sometimes, it seems to me that public indifference to poetry may free the poet from excessive restraint. They'll ignore me anyway, he'll say, so I'll do my own thing.

It seems possible that while poems 'ought not to be phantoms', they might still be trip-wires to those parallel worlds which live in our unconscious. If one is to say only what one means (or thinks one means) then perhaps poetry is not the best medium to say it in. Poetry is expedition rather than presentation, as even the more aphoristic poets prove. It is a paradigm of Free Will: at every juncture the writer may choose the path which leads to his ultimate goal—a lasting work of art. If Moses had been a poet, his Decalogue would have run differently: he would have been more interested in the shape of his Commandments than in their efficacy. This suggests that God is no poet either, except in his work of bringing order out of chaos and his instinct for drama, setting men at loggerheads by establishing individual conscience. Parallel invention is my term for what poetry does. The forces moving in the poet's mind may choose vents of utterance which are far removed from those they would use if their purpose were a press release or a policy statement. Thus the poet stands out in the verbal *diluvium universale*, and sends out his trained doves. What they bring back will not be known to him in advance.

But then comes another exemplary text from Enright. His poem 'Reflections on Foreign Literature' adds a particularized warning against exoticism to his previous warnings against obscurity— or, more accurately, against trying to make one's work profound by keeping it murky. This is the second part of the poem:

I remember my friend's friend, a barmaid in Shinjuku, at a literary pub—
Neither snowy-skinned nor sloe-eyed (though far from slow-witted),
Neither forward nor backward, of whom my friend
(A former PEN delegate) said in a whisper:
'Her life-story would make a book. I shall tell you one day . . .'
The day never came. But I can imagine the story.

My friend's friend also made special ties out of leather;
My friend gave me one, as a parting gift, a special memory of his country.
It has an elegant look; but when I wear it, it chafes my skin;
Whispering that nothing is exotic, if you understand, if you stick your
   neck out for an hour or two;
That only the very worst literature is foreign;
That practically no life at all is.

(CP, 50)

Earlier in the poem, Enright asks 'Do I live in foreign countries/Because they cannot corrupt me?', and adds the epigrammatic observation, 'The exotic: a rest from meaning'. This last statement is at the heart of my dilemma. I admit that it is the tyranny of meaning which drives me mad, and from which

I flee into various doubtful resorts, such as the spouting of oracles and the music of contradiction. I don't think I have ever deliberately written a line devoid of meaning, but this is a tribute to the robust syntax of our language. I have wanted to; I have lusted after the opaque armour of the hermeticists, and the glamorous Mallarméan white-out. And I am attracted to those poets who preserve the shapeliness of the classical past but add to it the excitement of experiment and mystery, to Rimbaud, Mallarmé, Stevens, and Ashbery. But I am drawn also to another sort of poet whose obscurity is due to his sheer intellect and originality, such as Auden was when he was young, and William Empson throughout his productive life. From time to time Enright himself finds too much sanity hard to bear:

> (You may think it is easy, all this sanity?
> Try it. It will send you mad.)
>
>   .   .   .   .
>
> This blue-eyed moderation is cold and hurtful
> To sensitive native.
>
>   .   .   .   .
>
> Do not complain,
> In this world you have no alibi.
> You disagreed with history, now history disagrees with you.
> 'Guilty' — plead this — 'guilty but sane.'
> Bar-girls are adoring the grand madmen, the police
> Wave them on with quiet but burning pride.
> Your nerves are twitching with sanity,
> Like an epileptic you throw yourself down on
> Clutch and brake and floor.
> Look —
>
>   ('Doctor Doctor', CP, 75–6)

In practice, Enright listens to more than just the voice of reason. His *Collected Poems* is rich in a confusion of sounds which echoes in the mind of an erudite exile, a reasonable Englishman observing the exotic worlds of Egypt, Germany, Japan, Thailand, and Singapore. There is nothing exotic in Enright's response to the countries he has lived in, but he never denies the Babel of their sites and ambience. Enright the rationalist may not guess how different his work is from that of the majority of his generation who stayed home. He has had to interpret the uninterpretable in order to keep faith with his poetic credo. It is no surprise therefore that many of his poems are indeed 'sad ires', and that he has become one of the most redoubtable defenders of the concept of irony in modern literature. The ironist may feel things more strongly than the positivist, which is why he is unpopular in these days of mystagoguery and theory-mongering. Enright loves to trope old legends—*Paradise Illustrated* and *A Faust Book*—and the effect is like those swarming frescoes on the walls of Italian churches, originally intended to introduce an illiterate public to the stories of the Bible: I am thinking especially of the interpretations of both Old and New Testament in the Collegiate Church, San Gimignano. Those Trecento painters meant nothing ironical, of course, but Enright's variations have the same sharp outline and pictorial probing which the Sienese delighted in. The more one reads Enright's poetry the more convinced one becomes that his hostility to obscurity is a sort of whistling to keep his spirits up. Even *The Terrible Shears* soon breaks out of its documentary plainness into an unexpected shock of the ordinary. The whole Enright *œuvre* trembles with suppressed strangeness: it is a journey into the wilderness of the human spirit. His poetry listens to sounds, at home and abroad, which are foreign to our ease and comfort. This is what makes it so powerful and so attractive to come back to.

Nevertheless, Enright is a characteristic English-speaker, interpreting the world of foreign sounds through the ear of a post-Imperial teacher. He is also an adept of German Literature. He might be expected to have some sympathy for such as myself on whose hearing both German and Italian fell Caliban-like in adolescence. I was less well-educated than Enright, but I probably had a little more money to play about with when I was in my teens and early manhood. He read voraciously in libraries; I bought records. German and Italian were the languages which wooed me, simply because they are the tongues in which the great masterpieces of European music are written. So it was that before I could read a word of German or Italian (I had been taught French at school, and Latin primitively) I listened for hours to recordings—*Le Nozze di Figaro, Die Zauberflöte, Don Giovanni, Die Schöne Mullerin*—without benefit of libretti or scores. We had to import these records in sets of 78s from England, and they arrived long before their accompanying explanations. To this day

I cannot hear the words properly, since my soul is set to listen to what it thought it heard then. The effect made by a first experience may be like a crinkle which sets a wave in the hair — thereafter the hair will go no other way. We had endured the English singing versions which ruled before the war — 'Now your days of philandering are over' for Figaro's 'Non piu andrai', and 'When a maiden takes your fancy' for Osmin's 'Wer ein Liebchen hat gefunden'. Now we were on our own, listening to English / Australian (John Brownlee, the finest Don Giovanni of his age) / American / German voices singing Italian, and an equally mixed team singing in German. The power of these first experiences is immensely strong.

My life as Caliban could go on forever. Even when a singer was performing in his own language, the confusion could be as great. The Constant Lambert recording of *Dido and Aeneas* was my introduction to Purcell's opera. The duet 'Fear no danger to ensue / The hero loves as well as you' might have been in Serbo-Croat for all I could make of it. And, more to the point, however well we know the words of operas, songs, and oratorios we hear them as musically-bedecked syllables. Some composers, Stravinsky most notably, prefer their words heard that way. By the same token, the great poems of the English language find themselves broken up in peoples' minds into half-remembered assemblies of sounds, into garlands of memorable phrases and strings of famous quotations. The power of these fragments should not be underestimated. When they come from foreign languages they remind us of a strange fact which is paradoxically not at variance with the Platonic theory of the work of art as a reproduction of a perfect template — namely that what we make of the world inside our minds is a palimpsest, a temple assembled from precious stones and the most dubious *disjecta membra*. We are all, like Autolycus, 'snappers-up of unconsidered trifles'.

It's appropriate to end with a short expounding of the real meaning of Pentecost. After the tongues of fire in the upper room, the disciples were able to talk to anyone they met and be understood by them. The Pentecost story is the opposite in intent to that of the Tower of Babel, but there is nothing in it to suggest that the evangelizing was done in any other than the preachers' native tongues. It was the comprehension of the listeners which was in receipt of a miracle. Our version of Pentecost is a poetical form of 'speaking in tongues'. What wafts to us on Caliban's breeze is more beautiful in its own garb than it could be in translation. The miracle we must pray for is an improvement in our ability to understand other languages, even if not to be able to converse in them. The analogy with music is strong. The ear goes before the eye, and it may tell us more peculiar things than rationality can. I started this essay by quoting from the early stanzas of *Letter to Lord Byron*. Here, from the end of the poem, is another apposite quotation:

> I like Wolf's *Goethe-lieder* very much,
> But doubt if *Ganymed*'s appeal will touch—
> That marvellous cry with its ascending phrases—
> Capitalism in its later stages.

However, I doubt that Auden was right when he suggested that it was 'the sound' of foreign languages which Ezra Pound liked. The Cantos seem an obvious example of what happens when Pentecost turns into theocracy. The voices in Chinese, Provençal, laconic Yankee, medieval Italian, *et al* which rush like tempests through Pound's head are as much to be doubted as those which spoke to Joan of Arc. They could be from the Devil as readily as from the Lord. The trouble is that what was natural and carried on the wind has become prescriptive and *dirigiste*. We may stay sane on playfulness, or go mad with prophecy. And this is one lesson which Dennis Enright's poetry can teach us. Foreigners are not unlike us, but their languages are different from ours. The exotic is to be shunned, but we are not to expect that what is called for in Leamington Spa will command the same allegiance in Singapore. The Japanese are not full of the wisdom of Zen, but they live in a decorum unlike ours. We are entitled to wonder at the sheer variousness of things, but pain, joy, apprehension, love, and fear are universal. We must content ourselves with observing how similar and how unlike we all are. '*Fahrt*' does sound funny in English and 'Bevilacqua' will never really be 'Drinkwater.' So we go on listening to the sounds which creep by us on the waters. As the Russian observed of Guy Burgess in Gavin Ewart's poem 'Heaving Drinking', 'He was definitely a tractor'. But let Enright have the last word about the gentle pleasures of semantic cross-dressing, a form of one-Handke clapping, in 'I am a Bewohner of an Elfenbeinturm':

It seems I live in an ivory tower
Or if I am German (am I a German?)
An Elfenbeinturm is my abode.
Do I abide in an elephant's leg?
Am I a flea then, a Faustian *Floh*?

If I were Chinese (but then I am
Not, China is not in Europe as yet)
I might reside in a Jade Pavilion.
Were I a more dynamic dreamer
I might inhabit a marble hall.

But if I am German only in part
(My German is only partly good)
Perhaps I dwell in an elf's left leg.
Or Number 11 Leg Towers maybe—
It has the ring of authenticity.

That I live at some remove from life,
Its down-to-earthiness, its low *Geschmack*,
Is owing to lifts forever out of service,
Trash on the stairs, the price of real ale,
And (oh!) the cost of public transport.

But write to me (if you can spare the postage)
At Flea Flat, Leg Towers, Elephant and Castle,
And tell me about the real and earnest.
                                    (CP, 279)

Those Foreigners

JOHN BAYLEY

BROWSING as I often do through D. J. Enright's *Collected Poems*, I am fascinated by the way his eclectic genius has mixed up so many different idioms, ways of writing and feeling in different languages. The effect of this is subtle and mostly beneath the surface of the poems. How do so many foreign and interior lives metamorphose on the page so unmistakably into Enright's own personality; how, most particularly, does the German language and German poetry respond so equably to this metamorphosis into English?

Not an easy question, but an important one. Enright's style combines the literary with the domestically ordinary in such a way as we never see either predominating, or self-consciously demanding attention. He constructs no *personae* (until Faust), as Browning and Ezra Pound do in their poetry, nor is he in any way an obvious scholar-poet, like for instance John Heath-Stubbs. In fact he strikes me as the most obviously 'natural' poet of his generation. Contemporaries—Philip Larkin, for example—constructed their poems in a manner which, if successful, was certainly paradoxical: they (and Larkin especially) took a very great deal of trouble to set up the poem, and maybe months, or even years, to mature and complete it; but this went with a deliberately no-nonsense, debunking attitude to culture, learning, witty reference, exotic places, and foreign works of art. Larkin, in fact, and other poets in what is still sometimes called 'the Movement' (already discussed in this collection of essays) went to great lengths to be spontaneously contemptuous of 'art', acting the part of Lucky Jim in poems which Jim himself would never have had the skill or the patience to piece together, nor the undeclared wish, so evident in Larkin, to commemorate an experience by creating what secretly aspires to be a perfect work of art.

All this artifice in order to appear aggressively natural is as alien to Enright as was the verbal pyrotechnics of Dylan Thomas or of the 'Apocalypse' poets. The admirable thing about Enright's poems is the spirit in which they take themselves. They do not create a personality but express one with perfect ease, in all its shapeliness and sharpness of thought, curiosity, and humour. These qualities are the product of an intelligence formed by extensive acquaintance with foreign societies and foreign literatures, an acquaintance acquired and worn with complete unpretentiousness, and one which knows England and English literature all the better and more equably from knowing others. Enright's poetry never shows off its cosmopolitanism—is never arrogant; but it thrives on the challenge of unfamiliar habits, peoples, customs; and, above all, on the odd ways in which foreign poetry (Cavafy, Heine, Brecht) can be naturalized in English if it is not regarded as alien, but in the idiom of a poet as subtle as Enright, treated as a comfortable native way of speaking and thinking.

To take an example, not quite at random, from *Addictions*, the collection published in 1962. In a poem called 'In Memoriam', Enright tells a story, in fact, from Japan: he remembers a young Englishman

> who went there to teach
> (Uncertificated, but they took him) in Tokyo,
> This Englishman with a fine beard and a large and
> (It seemed) a healthy body.
>   And he married an orphan,
> A Japanese orphan (illegitimate child of
> A geisha—Japanese for 'a clever person'—and a
> ˌNumber of customers), who spoke no English and
> He spoke no Japanese. (But how clever they were!)
> For a year they were married. She said, half in Japanese,
> Half in English, wholly in truth: 'This is the first time
> I have known happiness.' (The Japanese are a
> Clever people, clever but sad.) 'They call it a
> Lottery,' he wrote to me, 'I have made a lucky dip.'
> (She was a Japanese orphan, brought up in a convent.)
> At the end of that year he started to die.
>
>   (CP, 49–50)

There are several notable things about this poem, apart from what is obviously most moving about it: its human story. The young man dies of cancer; the Japanese widow, 'having known a year's happiness with a / Large blue-eyed red-bearded foreign devil', goes back to her convent. The poem concludes:

> There is a lot of cleverness in the world, but still
> Not enough.

It is a conclusion with the ring of a Goethean moral to it, a moral fully and ironically anglicized; and the constant use made of parentheses throughout the poem presents us with a ghostly image of the subordinate clauses in German syntax. The precision is not that of 'poetry', but of a kind of personal speech naturally evolved from the sense of difference in language. The impression produced is indeed half in one language, half in another—'wholly in truth'. It could be said of poetry that in general it shows what its own language is most—and most uniquely—capable of, and it is because of this preconception that Enright has not seemed to some critics to write 'real poetry'. With such persons his invisible originality has been his undoing.

The language factor so strongly determinant in what he writes goes with that other impression I referred to, that a poem of his can, as it were, take time to stop being a poem in order to tell the reader something, and then resume its poetic form. This of course is a matter of impression, perhaps deliberately created, or at least, allowed. But the information about 'geisha' meaning 'a clever person', and the sense the poem gives us of two separate and different people, is like the information—curious, touching, or dreadful—conveyed in a letter or a leisurely conversation in a bar. Its lightness rejects the intensity inherent in the poetry of a single language, and is a process much more subtle than it may appear. Far off but unmistakable in the background of 'In Memoriam' is the tone we catch in some of Goethe's most characteristic poems, like his *Tagebuch* (*The Diary*) and the *Roman Elegies*, in one of which the poet imagines himself counting the beat of his hexameters on the smooth vertebrae of his mistress in bed. Information like that seems detached from—held apart from, but so added to—what the poet is doing elsewhere, a Goethean trick (if that is the word) which Enright has insensibly absorbed and made his own.

So that we read his poems for information, for comments about life that strike one as unpretentious, piercing, and original—in short, for their wisdom. Enright has always declined, in his

humorous way, to admit that such a thing as 'foreignness' has
any real existence, although he sees it may be tempting to fall
back on 'the exotic: a rest from meaning'. In 'Reflections on
Foreign Literature' he says:

> The stories which my friends compose are very sad.
> They border on the morbid (which, in the literatures
> Of foreign languages, we may licitly enjoy, for they cannot really
> Corrupt, any more than we can be expected to discriminate).
>
> (Sometimes I ask myself: Do I live in foreign countries
> Because they cannot corrupt me, because I cannot be
> Expected to make the unending effort of discrimination? . . .)

The conclusion is deceptively simple, but leaves us sure that the
'unending effort' has to be made:

> That only the very worst literature is foreign;
> That practically no life at all is.
>
> (CP, 50–1)

In Berlin, where he taught for a year, Enright was ill at ease. He
found it 'dull and deadening', and was alarmed by the 'good
public behaviour of the Germans'.* I can vouch for the uncanny
accuracy of his feel for the place not so long after the end of the
war. In 'Berlin Side-Streets' he adopts the tone of art in order
to make a specific point about the way in which art is sued and
clung to—an odiously convenient reassurance—in a situation
where living is meanly devoured by the shame and the knowledge
of guilt:

> Set on a bomb-site, this furniture store
> Displays each night, discreetly lighted,
> The same bedroom suite, in reduced Empire,
> Where lovers pause to take some moral thought,
> Sweet it may be, or maybe bitter.
> Then, the bare flank of a brand-new theatre,
> Deliberate art of a defeated power,
> In which the great emotions play in safety,
> Off the streets, in municipal safety.
>
> (CP, 51)

* *Memoirs of a Mendicant Professor*, chap. 6.

This is exactly what the new Germany began to feel like; and the tone conveys with equal exactness the uneasy mixture of desire and conventions involved. After the war, in Germany, art seemed both wholly irrelevant and logically necessary, something that must be re-established, like the sewage system, if civilization were to be rebuilt. It is this surreal sense that Enright exactly catches in the idea of the lovers' conscientious pause: the fact that it doesn't matter in art—above all not in this new municipal reconstructed art—whether the medicine is 'sweet' or 'bitter': both are harmless, well-separated from *wiederaufgebau* and the new economic miracle. The sigh of relief almost audible in the repeated 'safety' gives the German timbre to the inglorious aesthetics and civic respectabilities that are being recycled.

Germanness itself becomes uncanny in Enright's ambiance, because it is so lightly assimilated, never giving us (as the Germans themselves and people in general so often do) a guarded, careful, or measuring look. We feel at home with Enright as he crosses frontiers: that is the genial paradox of his ease with (never familiarity with) foreign people. As readers we may relax.

The unbuttoned idiom that Enright has evolved, and which is used for thinking aloud, continues right through his work. In the section of new poems of 1981, 'Pains' and 'Those First Moments' make interesting examples. In 'Pains':

> One of the peculiarities of the word 'soul',
> Musil remarks, is that young people cannot pronounce it
>   without laughing,
> And the middle-aged fight shy of it except in phrases like
> 'X has a noble soul' or, more commonly, 'Y has a base soul'.
> It is, as he says, 'distinctly a word for the elderly'—
> Many of whom prefer to talk to themselves.
>
> We must leave Musil aside, for he was not invariably
> Nor indisputably serious. He inclined to a chronic irony
> Which led to the downfall of the Austro-Hungarian Empire.
>
> How stands the empire of the soul?
>
>   (CP, 266–7)

Eventually in this poem, musing in an un-English syntax and with a German hexametric movement, Enright talks himself beyond 'the kind of irony responsible for the ruin / Of the Dual Monarchy'—the 'pains are one's own'—and he concludes:

> If the soul is uncertain, more slippery still is belief,
> Which we used to think simple, the stuff of a trenchant
>   sentence or two.

For Musil, what really mattered was not *die Seele* but the thing that its grand and pious sound had always really stood for—sex. Or rather, the whole extraordinary and complex fascination that goes with a full awareness of what that deadpan little word means in daily existence, in the rivers of consciousness. Enright enters fully into this dimension of Musil, which is more to be savoured in the latter's short stories than in *The Man Without Qualities*. In the poem that follows, 'Those First Moments', Enright imagines the soul and the body precariously and incongruously united by the kind of consciousness so memorably explored by Musil. Soul makes a certain suggestion to body as they lean over the embankment:

> The body slumps against low railings.
> Here's a fine fast-flowing river, hums the soul,
> Peering out of bleary eyes:
> Water answers several questions . . . washed and willing.
>
> The body straightens up, as if accosted.
> Easy on, the soul says, can't you take a joke?
> But neither laughs . . .

> (CP, 267–8)

Instead they go quietly home to take a bath together.

   A Faust Book is given an essay of its own in this book; it must be the culmination of Enright's involvement with German literature, and with Goethe in particular. There is of course a close connection between his admirable essays on Goethe's *Faust*, first published in the Forties in *Scrutiny*, the organ of his Cambridge tutor, F. R. Leavis, and his own poetic *Faust Book*, written over thirty years later. The academic jokes in *A Faust Book* are unsurpassed, but there is nothing esoteric about them. As one might expect, the account is full of the most normal, down-to-earth kinds of human experience, making explicit what is already implicit in the high style of Goethe's drama. 'I prefer true stories', says Justus, the son of Faust in Enright's sequence; so, perhaps, does the poet who thought of him. Enright's unassuming preference for truth comes out in all his work. In an earlier poem, 'The Accents of Brecht', he reflected on a time when 'Plain speaking was merely truth', and on the way these two concepts had become entangled. 'Who am I then to complain' if society can put paid to the accents of Brecht?

And so Enright both responds to, and sees through, the German *aesthetik*. Life for him is continually escaping from art, but not always in the expected direction. One of the short poems in *The Terrible Shears* unexpectedly introduces Thomas Mann's Faustus character, Leverkühn, as he gives his last address to a cultivated assembly. How relieved they were to find that this was 'poetry'! But then again, they found it wasn't, and went home indignant: 'They had expected an artistic soirée.'

A Faust Book

LEONARD FORSTER

ENRIGHT is the only person I can think of in the English literary world at the moment who, without ever having been a professional Germanist, has been consistently and productively devoted to the work of Goethe. He published a commentary on Goethe's *Faust* in *Scrutiny* in 1945 at the age of 25 (a thing no Germanist would have dared to do). Not many Germanists read *Scrutiny* in those days (they were too busy relearning the German they had forgotten on war service), and indeed it wasn't often that *Scrutiny* had anything for them, so his extremely perspicacious remarks passed unnoticed by the trade. They were reprinted by New Directions in 1949, and promptly submerged in the flood of Goethe literature that centenary year produced. Then, after thirty years of further reflection, the critic gave way to the poet, who wrote a different kind of commentary only a poet could write: *A Faust Book* (1979).

It looks at first sight like a lyric cycle, but on closer inspection the narrative element is seen to be strong, and then one realizes that each poem describes a scene, so that from a lyric cycle it becomes a series of dramatic tableaux capable of being presented on a stage.* The apparently simple form turns out to be surprisingly complex and flexible. It allows Enright to recreate the Faust story for our time. He does it not by straight narrative or dramatic presentation, but by a series of film shots which together make up a sort of *pointilliste* picture. (This odd combination of technical terms shows how elusive Enright's achievement is.) He had already tried out this technique on Milton in *Paradise Illustrated* which had appeared the previous year. Here too he employed verse, sometimes rhymed, sometimes unrhymed, sometimes using assonance; in *A Faust Book* he also employs prose on occasion. He draws on Goethe, Marlowe, Valéry, and the German

---

* As it was by the Rose Bruford College of Speech and Drama: *Faustplay: a show based on* A Faust Book *by D. J. Enright* (19 July 1983) at the National Poetry Centre, London.

and English chap-books (but not, as far as I can see, on any of
the operas—Gounod, Boito, Busoni, Berlioz), and evidently
expects his readers to have these works present in their minds.
Against this background he preserves an ironic detachment,
presenting familiar scenes in modern terms, using references
ranging from oblique allusion to direct parody. By virtue of this
detachment he is able to bring episodes from his predecessors
closer to us—often closer to us than we would like.

An adequate treatment of the relation between Enright's and
Goethe's *Faust* would need to be very extensive and cannot
be undertaken here. And there would need to be an equally
extensive treatment of Enright and Marlowe. But the Germanist
is particularly attracted by the echoes he hears of Goethe's *Faust*,
and Enright's cycle begins with one. Marlowe and Goethe had
begun with a tremendous dramatic-lyric monologue. Enright
wisely avoids this and begins with the Easter walk from Goethe,
with Faust picking up the poodle (or vice versa). This is a reference
only; Enright throughout skilfully avoids direct comparison with
famous set-pieces, except in a few cases we shall consider later.

Enright's Faust remains throughout the Wittenberg professor
(he had had young Hamlet as a pupil); we are even introduced
to SCR and High-Table gossip, the Rector and the Rector's wife.
No classical Greece (but Helen!), no Walpurgisnacht, classical
or modern, no Emperor's Court (but the Duke of Parma from the
chap-book), no draining of the fens, no descent to the Mothers.
In place of Philemon and Baucis we have Faust's parents from
the chap-book: decent working class, uncomprehending and
suspicious of the up-market life their clever son is leading in
a household consisting of himself, Gretchen, Mephisto, and
Meretrix. Meretrix (merry tricks) a 'go-go dancer' and a lively
character, is a new face. She has no parallel in Goethe or Marlowe,
but one feels that she is what Frau Marthe once was or would
have liked to be, and it is significant that she comes out tops in
the end. Enright has avoided the temptation of making his scope
too wide ('Wir sehn die kleine, dann die grosse Welt'); but though
the scene is a small university town there are supernal (and
infernal) dimensions to it. No Prologue in Heaven but a couple
of interludes in Hell, with Lucifer himself speaking out of a
cloud like God in the Bible (e.g. Luke 9: 35). Faust senses God
meditating in the Harz (in contrast to Goethe's Walpurgisnacht

on the Brocken); Mephisto remembers the face of God; Lucifer broods. Faust's political achievements, so important to Goethe, are treated ironically: 'Thus Faust did good, as he had wanted, and / Little good came of it', thus reversing Mephisto as 'ein Teil von jener Kraft Die stets das Böse will und stets das Gute schafft'. The irony reaches its height in the brilliant scene in which Mephisto plays the professor (as he had in Goethe's 'Schülerszene') lecturing on, of all things, the two final scenes of Goethe's *Faust II*. Characters from these scenes, the Blessed Boys (Goethe's 'Selige Knaben') had already made their appearance earlier on, to Mephistopheles's discomfiture; now they are the students to whom he is lecturing. The lecture is a washout . . .

Enright's Faust, like Goethe's, is saved at the end; not by virtue of any continuous striving but as the result of a strategic policy decision by Lucifer: 'throwing a sprat to catch a school of mackerel.' He lets the Doctor go free 'to encourage the others'. So Faust, instead of being a hero, an 'Übermensch', turns out to be a mere sprat, not even a cog in the machinery of infernal planning; one wonders what all the fuss was about. Mephistopheles indeed does just that; in Valéry he thinks: 'Il se peut que je ne serve à rien.' In Enright, 'sometimes he wondered / Who he was working for' ('. . . und stets das Gute schafft').

Where does that leave them all? Liberated Faust decides to pass his time in 'some far wilderness'—surely an echo of the last scene of *Faust II*—where he will find other hermits ('Was there no wilderness at hand?'). Wagner gets a job at Heidelberg 'coaching some student princeling' (the reference here is to Wilhelm Meyer-Förster's immensely successful sentimental play *Alt-Heidelberg* (1901), filmed by Lubitsch in 1927 as *The Student Prince*; he will inherit Faust's gold watch. Faust's parents, too, are named in his will. Gretchen lives 'far off', and just to show there is no ill-feeling, she is bequeathed Faust's second-best bed, like Anne Hathaway. Meretrix comes off best; she inherits Faust's worldly goods as residuary legatee. (There must be a moral here somewhere . . .)

The great questions remain unanswered: why the guiltless suffer and why the wicked thrive. Lucifer plans for the future, hoping to catch a school of mackerel with Faust as sprat. God is working out his purpose, for 'Creation is never finished'.

What has all the fuss about knowledge and experience amounted to? To the realization that Faust is in spite of everything a very unimportant, self-regarding person, not really worth Mephistopheles's highly qualified time, when all is said and done. '*How wide is all this long pretence?*' we may ask with George Herbert.* At the moment of signing the pact, Faust knows the answer: '*There is in love a sweetnesse readie penn'd: / Copie out onlie that, and save expense.*' Marlowe's Faustus is the new man of the Renaissance, Goethe's Faust the type of, struggling mankind; Marlowe, Goethe, and Thomas Mann (all of whom Enright greatly admires) between them have made Faust one of the great European cult figures, embodied in splendid language and arousing countless associations, much larger than life. Enright's spare, understated, down-to-earth poetry, couched in flat colloquial speech rhythms, behind which lie irony and humour, deflates this legendary figure and cuts him down to size, but in so doing brings him nearer to people of our time. It is worth looking at a couple of examples of how he does it.

'Faust and Gretchen walk in the garden' is parallel to 'Marthens Garten' in Goethe's *Faust I* with the famous discussion about religion, Gretchen asking the simple penetrating questions ('Glaubst du an Gott?') and Faust giving evasive answers. Goethe makes Faust's answers important statements of genuine belief (his own at the time); Enright shows Faust side-stepping the whole thing by using typical intellectual double-talk, the familiar tactics of the philosophy tutorial:

> 'Can anyone say he believes in God?
> What is meant by *God*?
> What is meant by *believe*?
> What is meant by *I*?
> Can we employ these words any more?'
> (CP, 224)

Goethe's Gretchen replies to his rhapsodic credo: 'Ungefähr sagt das der Pfarrer auch, / Nur mit ein bisschen anderen Worten'; Enright's Gretchen is similarly rooted in faith and feels that she *can* employ these questionable words ('Though in fact she rarely did'). His Faust leaves the giddy heights of philosophy and kisses

* 'Jordan', from *The Temple*.

Gretchen's hand, as Goethe's had in a previous scene. Enright's Gretchen, like Goethe's, distrusts Mephisto. His Faust, like Goethe's, gives Gretchen jewellery, a crucifix she wears round her neck, the loss of which is symbolic. It is a down-to-earth, everyday gift, unlike the 'Kästchen . . . und Sachen Herrlich ganz und gar' she receives in Goethe, though both came from Mephisto. Enright plays down and makes the whole scene ironic ('Actually I'm a Doctor of Divinity myself') but it remains moving and dramatically effective in its new form. He has condensed into a page-and-a-half (37 short lines) three whole scenes of Goethe's play; brilliant as these scenes are, they even seem, by contrast, a trifle portentous and verbose; not what one usually has occasion to think about Goethe.

'Gretchen at the sewing-machine' parallels 'Gretchen am Spinnrade'. Schubert's marvellous setting makes us forget that what Goethe wrote was not a song but a dramatic monologue. And so it is appropriate that Enright's poem cannot be sung to Schubert's music. 'Gretchen am Spinnrade' takes place before her seduction by Faust, 'Gretchen at the sewing-machine' after it. It rewrites Goethe's monologue in the light of Gretchen's other great monologues in 'Zwinger', 'Dom', and the scene with Lieschen, 'Am Brunnen'. By skilful oblique reference Enright has concentrated these four scenes into one.

The sewing-machine puts the scene in our day. The scene in the other poems is timeless; there are no modern props like aircraft, radio, computers, and so on, but here we are brought down to modern times and realize that a spinning-wheel would have no place in Enright's scenery. But why the sewing-machine rather than a washing-machine? (We know Gretchen is 'a dab at wash tub and flat iron'.) Surely because she is making a garment for the child she is expecting, and this situation is brutally stated in the first lines of Enright's poem; Goethe's love-longing has become despair. The contrast is carried through with rhythmical brilliance, the conciseness of expression following Goethe's own, and the ruthlessness is impressive. Germans with whom I have discussed this poem were deeply shocked by it; they felt it to be something in the nature of sacrilege, for Gretchen too is a cult figure. I felt and still feel that it is the high point of the whole cycle. The bleakness of the last stanza is impressive in itself:

'My stomach is swelling,
My peace is fled,
I wish I'd been careful,
I wish I was dead.'
                    (CP, 248)

and it is enhanced if one has in mind the lines it is parodying.

Goethe's Gretchen dies in prison, having killed her child, but is reunited with Faust in Heaven. Enright's Gretchen finds a down-to-earth, doubtless makeshift solution; she evidently did not have an abortion or a miscarriage but 'lived far off, with a man who wanted children' (and who perhaps did not mind too much if the first child was not his), and so disappears from view. One begins to suspect that the simple girl Gretchen who 'has a large soul and small breasts' is ultimately more important than the strutting self-absorbed Faust. God has her in mind and fashions 'a special measure / For the likes of Gretchen, a still sad music', which is more than he ever does for Faust. No drama, nothing sublime, just something everyday. (*There is in love a sweetnesse readie penn'd.*')

Enright avoids heroics; that is his great contribution to the development of the Faust theme. In his *Commentary on Faust* (p. 141) he speaks of 'the constant effort to bring his theme out of the philosopher's study and into the arena of actual human living which Goethe makes (with varying success) all through his larger works'. He has taken it a stage further.

Hearing about Damnation
The Collected Poems*

DONALD DAVIE

IN 1957, reviewing D. J. Enright's *Bread Rather than Blossoms* (for all practical purposes his second collection of poems), I exhorted him to remember 'the deeper reaches (and so the deeper humanity) of the art he practises'. I wish I saw clearer evidence in his *Collected Poems* that he noticed this exhortation, or thought it worth attending to. On the other hand, this observation is not so dismissive as it sounds. And in any case, I was ungracious earlier on in not acknowledging that Enright had already showed that he could navigate those deeper waters if he wanted to. The proof was, and is, in the title-poem, of his first collection, 'The Laughing Hyena, by Hokusai', which I must first have encountered in G. S. Fraser's anthology, *Poetry Now* (1956). It reappeared that same year in Robert Conquest's anthology, *New Lines*, and I fear I did not recognize in it — as I do now — perhaps the finest poem in that volume, and certainly the most surprising. It is well known, but it isn't *famous*, as it deserves to be. Much of it is written in long looping lines that can't be tucked into the usual type-panel, or into the margins of even wide pages. These long lines were to become one of Enright's hallmarks, but in later poems they are not often so splendidly justified. Here they generate looping and leaping rhythms which enact equivalent effects in the different medium of Hokusai, for whom, we are told, 'everything was molten', whose kite 'soars like sacrificial smoke', with whom

> All is flux: waters fall and leap, and bridges leap and fall.
> Even his Tortoise undulates . . .
>
> (CP, 13)

Enright's language leaps and falls and undulates in sympathy, with an energy that is, like Hokusai's 'volcanic':

---

* This article, now only lightly edited, first appeared as a review of the *Collected Poems*, in the *London Review of Books*, 3–16 Dec. 1981.

And the Laughing Hyena, cavalier of evil, as volcanic as the rest:
Elegant in a flowered gown, a face like a bomb-burst,
Featured with fangs and built about a rigid laugh,
Ever moving, like a pond's surface where a corpse has sunk.

Between the raised talons of the right hand rests an object—
At rest, like a pale island in a savage sea—a child's head,
Immobile, authentic, torn and bloody—
The point of repose in the picture, the point of movement in us.

With that line, of course, we come up against the moral crux. The
movement prompted in us by a child's bloody head torn from
its body is a movement of horror. Or rather that is what it prompts
in us as soon as we take it out of Hokusai's composition, where
on the contrary, it is 'the point of repose'. Is this tolerable? Can
we allow art thus to impose itself on us, so as to annul and even
reverse the nausea and outrage which stir in us as soon as we
step outside the aesthetic frame? This is the crux in poem after
poem by Enright, and mostly he resolves it by saying in effect:
'No. This is intolerable. I will not tolerate it, will not tolerate art
on these terms.' But in this early poem he solves the crux the
other way:

Terrible enough, this demon. Yet it is present and perfect,
Firm as its horns, curling among its thick and handsome hair.
I find it an honest visitant, even consoling, after all
Those sententious phantoms, choked with rage and uncertainty,
Who grimace from contemporary pages. It, at least,
Knows exactly why it laughs.

Here, for what I think is the one and only time in Enright's career,
he finds himself able to accept that art, at any rate some great
art, is amoral, unleashing energies which do not stop short of,
which may even *seek out*, gratuitous ferocities. I fear that when
with too much aplomb I urged him to plumb the 'deeper reaches',
I had myself not taken account of the sharks and barracuda which
swim in those depths. For I too, like Dennis Enright, though a
few years later, had been schooled by F. R. Leavis in Cambridge,
to believe that the energies behind worthwhile art were moral
energies, and accordingly that it was dangerous and wrong
to think of the aesthetic as a distinct category, where moral
judgements were, or might have to be, suspended.

This poem as I now read it records Enright's encounter with the furious energies of a great artist, an encounter which compels him, at least for the moment, to abandon that reassuring Leavisite conviction. Indeed, he not only encounters Hokusai, but he is sucked into Hokusai's energetic vortex, as we can tell from the energies released in his own language; and so the conclusion in Hokusai's favour was inevitable if the poet was to be honest.

Enright, however, is deeply humane, indeed humanitarian—too much so, if not for his own good, for the good of his art. Or so we may think. Accordingly, in later years, when confronting the apparently unavoidable inhumanity of art, he usually by the plainest implication refuses the bargain—as for instance in 'A Polished Performance', which was first published in *New Lines—2* (1963):

> Citizens of the polished capital
>   Sigh for the towns up country,
> And their innocent simplicity.
>
> People in the towns up country
>   Applaud the unpolished innocence
> Of the distant villages.
>
> Dwellers in the distant villages
>   Speak of a simple unspoilt girl,
> Living alone, deep in the bush.
>
> Deep in the bush we found her,
>   Large and innocent of eye,
> Among gentle gibbons and mountain ferns.
>
> Perfect for the part, perfect,
>   Except for the dropsy
> Which comes from polished rice.
>
> In the capital our film is much admired,
>   Its gentle gibbons and mountain ferns,
> Unspoilt, unpolished, large and innocent of eye.
>   (CP, 36)

This is much nearer to a typical 'Movement' poem. And the difference between this and 'The Laughing Hyena' is presumably what the jacket of the cloth edition had in mind when it invited us to notice that 'D. J. Enright's style has developed from the sensuous and extravagant formalities of some of his early poems into the pared-down referential wit of his later work.' This seems right, and is phrased with some nicety. But what has been left behind in the Hokusai poem, along with the sensuousness and the formal extravagance, is *energy*. No long lines here, no mounting and coiling and leaping rhythms, but clipped and ironic distance; Enright ensures that none of us are going to encounter this film except on his terms, certainly we are not to be 'caught up' in it, as he was caught up by and into the composition of Hokusai. I'm not sure he doesn't suggest that if we go to see this film, we should be ashamed of ourselves.

One of the questions asked about the Movement poets is whether, taken one by one, they have 'developed' (and, if they haven't, whether and how much this matters). There can be no doubt about Enright: he has 'developed' all right, and with awesome consistency. Thus from the distrust of art's autonomy that we find in 'A Polished Performance' and other poems like it, there is a straight, inflexible line to what we read in the autobiographical sequence, *The Terrible Shears*:

> Now I could watch unmoved the casting
> Of hundreds of books into dustbins.
> But two of them I think I should still
> Dive in after—Shakespeare and the Bible.
> (CP, 133)

This is development indeed!—especially for those like me who first read D. J. Enright (supposing him much older than myself) in the pages of *Scrutiny*, patiently explaining to us Rilke or Goethe. So much more widely read than most of us, he finds himself compelled by the logic of his own *decency*, his humane indignations, to a point where he would salvage, out of all the books he has read, just two. It was an inevitable outcome; but most of us would cravenly have contrived, one way or another, to shuffle out of the logic of our own convictions. Not he! And one is indignant at the many who compliment him on his decency without counting the sacrifices that his decency has exacted of him. For there is no way to turn aside this protestation by pretending that Enright is here speaking in character or through a *persona*—something that can be managed for instance with Larkin's notorious 'Books

are a load of crap'. Enright knows all about *personae*, but he'll have
no truck with them, certainly not in *The Terrible Shears*. This is
what must be meant by '*referential* wit'. It is what other voices,
for instance French ones, might call disparagingly 'anecdotal'.
Enright knows all about that sort of disparagement; he consistently
invites it and defies it. For him the content, the subject-matter,
must always have precedence over the style, the 'treatment';
because only by thus relegating treatment to secondary status can
he be sure of denying to his art the autonomy that he knows it
is always seeking for.

And so in *The Terrible Shears* one is continually aghast at the
tight rein he keeps on his art, the frugality he imposes on it.
Certainly *The Terrible Shears* is in verse; and one even concedes
that the harrowing record could not have been done except
in verse (its clipped cadences shutting out any self-pity, any
rhetorical elaboration). As a pitilessly unsensational chronicle of
what a working-class childhood could be in the England of the
1920s, it is irreplaceable. But is it in any real sense *poetry*? And
from where I stand I have to judge that it isn't, because all its
devices of language are quite plainly *instrumental*—they serve,
and they subserve, the subject-matter; whatever energies are
released are (quite deliberately) released by the theme, not at
all by the medium, never from within language. Accordingly
the admission that only two books in English are ultimately
worth saving must be taken, I think, quite literally, as a sincere
profession of considered opinion. Enright, to be sure, goes on
trafficking in literature—for instance as reviewer (and a very good
one); still, we can save him from inconsistency by supposing that
Shakespeare and the Bible make up all of literature that matters to
him *whenever he remembers his own and his parents' life in Leamington
fifty or sixty years ago*. For them, as for the overworked bar-girls
in post-war Japan, literature and the other arts were most of the
time luxuries that they could not (emotionally) afford. Enright
never forgets that, and won't let us forget it. Which is admirable
of him, and has been duly admired, though not more than it
deserves. All the same, *is* this the acid-test that should be applied
to the artist? It is a shame that penurious people in Leamington
Spa in the 1920s could not afford to partake of Art at all often.
But is that Art's fault? Surely the blame lies elsewhere: neither
with them, nor with the Art that mostly can't speak to them.

Along these lines one begins to think that the harsh Either / Or on which Enright has impaled himself—either 'subject' *or* 'treatment', either Truth *or* Art—is in fact negotiable, in ways he has refused to contemplate. And if so, the French sneer, 'anecdotal', has substance and force—as applied to Enright's poems, but also (and more) to British poetry generally through now several decades.

Was there ever a poet so 'responsible'? Enright never lets himself off the hook, but is always reminding himself what is owed to the things and people he writes about, and to the people who will read him. Much as we may admire civic and moral responsibility in our writers, surely in Enright's case it is excessive; for not just in *The Terrible Shears* but in his poems more generally one feels that the pressure of these responsibilities has left him too little room for manœuvre, too little margin for invention and caprice. One of the responsibilities that he recognizes is to be always entertaining. And whether or not other responsibilities irk him, this one certainly does—there is a remarkable, savagely snarling poem called 'Monkey' which says as much. It is this determination to be entertaining—jokey, and quotable—which tends to obscure the most interesting development in Enright through recent years: from the aesthete to the moralist, yes, but then from the moralist into something else—from secular humanism into religion. We notice this first in his fifth collection, *The Old Adam* (1965), which lives up to the promise of its title in being steadily concerned with Original Sin.

'A Liberal Lost', 'Visiting', and 'Misgiving at Dusk' are other pieces from this collection that tell the same story, and in the last of these—as William Walsh also points out—this new preoccupation recovers energy and intensity in language:

> Shaking with lust, the mosquitoes
> Stiffen themselves with bloody possets.
> I have become their stews.

(CP, 71)

Thereafter, every few pages, we find poems worrying away at points of Christian doctrine, particularly the bleakest of them, the doctrine of the Fall. In *Daughters of Earth* there is 'The Faithful', a rewriting of Hardy; 'More Memories of Underdevelopment', rewriting Hopkins; 'How Many Devils Can Dance on the

Point . . .', tracing the Calvinist logic of Cowper, whose 'God moves in a mysterious way' is to be just under the surface of other poems; and in particular there is 'Children Killed in War', which seems to be a self-accusing revision of the early and inadequate Dylan Thomas imitation, 'On the Death of a Child', but is also in part a rewriting of Yeats, contending that the unjust killing of children requires for its comprehension a dimension beyond the humanistic. In *Sad Ires* there is the very powerful 'Stations of King's Cross', and 'The Cauldron', along with at least five more poems turning on Christian dogma. And in the twenty-eight new poems (1981) that round out this *Collected Poems*, at least half, by my count, answer to the same description. As for the two long sequences, *Paradise Illustrated* and *A Faust Book*, the titles speak for themselves; although in both the tone is mocking, the mockery is not at the expense of the Christian myth, the sombre *fable*, which on the contrary is presented as compellingly plausible.

To be sure, all these pieces could be read, and no doubt they most often are, as more or less raucously blasphemous. But one does not blaspheme that which one has no belief in—a familiar and irrefutable argument, which Enright himself rehearses in the last lines of 'The Cauldron'. We may think of how Peter de Vries repeatedly reconsiders and vindicates his ancestral Dutch Calvinism in a series of hilariously bawdy novels which are commonly taken to be only entertainments—'screamingly funny' (as indeed they are). Comedy, in the hands of such as Enright and De Vries, is a very serious *genre*.

And what about Enright's most confessional work, *The Terrible Shears*? If he has become a religious poet, surely the proof of his having done so must be somewhere among the afflictions and desolations there bitterly, though still jokily, remembered. And indeed the proof is there—in pieces like 'Sunday', but pre-eminently in a poem carefully placed in this sequence about Leamington even though it seems to belong quite elsewhere. It takes its start from Thomas Mann's *Doctor Faustus*:

> As Leverkühn began his last address
> To the cultivated ladies and gentlemen
> There assembled,
> They were highly bewildered.

Till one of them cried,
'Why, it is poetry! One is hearing poetry!'
Thus relieving them all immensely.

But not for long—
As the composer's friend noted—
Alas, not for long did one think so!
They were hearing about damnation.

It sent the speaker mad.
The listeners it sent home indignant.
They had expected an artistic soirée.

(CP, 142)

For many years now, what we have been hearing about from Enright is damnation: not in the hereafter of course, but *now*. Such is the price you pay for keeping sedulously (responsibly) in touch with your reader; he forces you to inhabit, in full consciousness, the hell that he inhabits without knowing it.

A Sense of Religion
Enright's God

A. S. BYATT

'STRANGE that a sense of religion should/Somehow survive all this grim buffoonery!', reflects D. J. Enright, recalling his childhood Sundays in *The Terrible Shears*. That 'sense' did survive and indeed is pervasive, in his poetry. In the more recent *Instant Chronicles*, the 'short thoughts' include:

> Quite often heard to call on God—
> Though not expecting an answer.
>
> For who else could he call on—
> On some temporal lord and master?
>
> Angry with the one for being there;
> With the other for not, still angrier.
> (CP, 317)

Anger with God for being absent is one form of the Enright religion. Sometimes it appears that God was once there, and good, as in the poem 'High-mindedness of an English Poet' which takes on the advocate of Job-like patience in modern politics.

> Job is the case he cites
> Whose readiness to sing
> Under the frequent scourge
> Was a fine and sacred thing—
> But God was living then,
>
> And you and I, my dear,
> Seeing the bad go free
> The good go by default
> Know more than one sole state
> Where this sweet bard would be
> Appointed laureate.
> (CP, 117)

This sense of the past existence of a good God is, however, comparatively rare. (Christ is different; we come to Him later.) Anthropos, feeling his age, also feels the death of God, but more as a loss of a sense of profundity in things. He has fewer things to hide from we are told. Religions are not supposed to burn him:

> . . . Once there were torrents to cross,
> Forests to explore, and the nature of God.
> The objects that squat on his desk
> Afford him no refuge.
>
> (CP, 205–6)

The demonologizing of the desk-things is akin to much of the peculiar, not quite malign energy of modern non-mysterious objects in the most recent poems, such as 'Psalm for Supersunday'.

The nature and origin of Enright's argument with God can be discerned, directly and obliquely, in *The Terrible Shears*. There is a kind of sociological picture of accepted religion, its tedium and its fears and puzzles that most of us who are old enough will remember, working-class or not. The God of this world is a Sunday God, and the Sundays on which the child goes to Sunday School and the Church are seen, ironically, as at best, God's time off.

> It was a far cry from that brisk person
> Who created the heaven and the earth in
> Six days and then took Sunday off.
>
> (CP, 133–4)

The tone of the description of the Sunday School is childish mockery and adult pity and indignation mixed:

> In Sunday school a sickly adult
> Taught the teachings of a sickly lamb
> To a gathering of sickly children.

Nevertheless it is at the end of this poem that Enright remarks on the strange persistence of a 'sense of religion', and concludes 'Perhaps that brisk old person does exist/And we are living through his Sunday.' Connected to this sense of Sunday emptiness, as opposed to fullness, is the child's inability to respond to the masses of flowers in the town's gardens, admission free on Sundays. They 'were emblematic/Of something, I couldn't make out what'. They press round him, muttering 'too softly for me to hear':

> I never learnt their true names.
> If I looked at them now,
> I would only see the sound of Sunday church bells.
>   (CP, 127)

The effect here of Sunday is, as so often in these poems, both muffling and deadening, and obscurely enlivening at the same time. The flowers never come to life in terms of the Pathetic Fallacy, but their Sundayness has its vitality.

The accounts of people are both comic and terrible, often both at once, depending on how seriously we take religion at all. The poet's mother is Protestant and has a Protestant mistrust of the religion of his father, a 'lapsed Catholic'.

> My mother's strongest religious feeling
> Was that Catholics were a sinister lot;
> She would hardly trust even a lapsed one.
> My father was a lapsed Catholic.
>   (CP, 133)

Here the word 'lapsed' carries also the weight of Enright's sense, wholly informing the language and the shape of the poems, of man's fallen nature. (Remember the Voice of the Bard, in the *Songs of Experience*, 'Calling the lapsed soul'.) Various short poems in this sequence enact the Fall, obliquely, ironically. Consider 'The Soul of a Schoolboy':

> A woman thrust her way into the house,
> Desirous to save the soul of a schoolboy.
>
> An obliging schoolboy, would do anything
> For peace, excepting kneel in public.
>
> But no, she would not go, she would not go,
> Till crack on their knees they fell together.
> His soul was lost forever.
>   (CP, 150)

This is an anecdote, but it somehow makes us both smile and see the riddling weight of the words. 'Anything for peace' is embarrassed or evangelical. 'They fell together' neatly reverses the blundering evangelist's intention, and precisely. They fell *together*. Both sin. And the 'crack' is descriptive, and a Mephistophelean firework.

Equally succinct and full of import is the little poem, 'Two Bad Things in Infant School':

> Learning bad grammar, then getting blamed for it:
> Learning Our Father which art in Heaven.
>
> Bowing our heads to a hurried nurse, and
> Hearing the nits rattle down on the paper.
> (CP, 123)

Here God, as throughout Enright's poems, is associated with language and fallen language. Our Father *which* art in Heaven has something grammatically wrong with it. Juxtaposition involves the blame for the grammar in the saying of the prayer. 'God is a harsh master, who put his creatures in the way of damning themselves and then went on damning them,' said Enright in his Introduction to his selection from *Paradise Lost*.* And the bowed head from which the nits fall is a secular bowing which echoes the prayer, comic, yes, but spreading into meaning, because the nits rattle down, they fall, like the sinful. Even the idea of paper connects the prayer to the written language, and the nits to bad words.

And the involvement of religion with language and eventually with poetry, for Enright, is seen in the poems, 'A Sign' and 'It Is Poetry'. In 'A Sign' the young poet retrieves an old broken-backed Bible from the dustbin, describing his scandalized look, and restraint from chiding these 'blasphemers against God's Word'. He makes it quite clear what was sacred to *him*:

> At that tender age I couldn't bear
> To see printed matter ill treated.
> I would have subscribed to the ancient
> Oriental taboo against stepping light-
> Mindedly over paper inscribed with characters.
> (CP, 133)

---

* *A Choice of Milton's Verse*, Faber and Faber, 12.

His impressed elders see the episode in terms of religion:

> It was read as a sign. The child
> Is destined to become Vicar of the Parish Church!
> He has rescued Religion from the scrap-heap.

But the poet does not leave us with the contrast between his true respect for print and his supposed respect for religion. Now, he tells us, he could watch unmoved the casting of hundreds of books into dustbins. But would still dive in after Shakespeare and the Bible. And the Bible retains its ambivalent significance.

The poem 'It Is Poetry' seems at first to sit oddly in this sequence between a poem which begins 'Grandma doddered a bit, / But she was my friend,' and one about the gym teacher. It concerns the damned artist of Thomas Mann's *Doctor Faustus*, Leverkühn, and describes his 'last address / To the cultivated ladies and gentlemen'; these hearers are at first relieved to diagnose what he is saying as 'poetry' and then disturbed to realize they were 'hearing about damnation'.* The poem treats damnation and European literature, two preoccupations of the adult Enright, and is placed where it is *because* it follows the extremely painful, if fiercely understated, description of the dispatch of Grandma to the Workhouse, which she feared. Enright asks,

> Perhaps it had to be done,
> Did it have to be done like that?

And he goes on to tell us:

> It started me writing poems,
> Unpleasant and enigmatic,
> Which quite rightly no one liked,
> But were thought to be 'modern'.
>   (CP, 142)

Here, in the juxtaposition of the local rage against the suffering of the helpless and the innocent, with high modernist art (*Doctor Faustus*) deriving from ancient myth and belief, is a kind of seed or paradigm of Enright's religious poetry.

One steady strand in it is a refusal to understand or accept the pain of the innocent, a refusal local and observed, as in the elegant

---

* This poem is quoted in full by Donald Davie, see p. 156, as is 'A Polished Performance', p. 152.

poem, 'A Polished Performance' about the large-eyed innocent girl, 'Perfect for the part', of a tourist attraction 'except for the dropsy / Which comes from polished rice'; but also connected to the theological anger of Ivan Karamazov, when Enright's Faust asks Mephistopheles 'Why is it little children suffer, / Guiltless beyond dispute?' and gets the bureaucratic and hellish answer:

> 'It passes understanding,'
>   came the pious answer.
> 'It may surprise you, but in hell
> We need to keep child-murderers and molesters
> Segregated from the rest. Feelings run high.'
>
> (CP, 220)

Because of his riddling tone of voice, matter of fact, funny and terrible, Enright can make us look at children in war, or depicted in the talons of Hokusai's 'Laughing Hyena, cavalier of evil', who holds

> a child's head
> Immobile, authentic, torn and bloody—
> The point of repose in the picture, the point of movement in us.
>
> (CP, 13)

Which says much about the relation of art to life, of what it is to be 'moved', of evil. In a coolly balanced early poem about the Chinese poets, he begins:

> Only one subject to write about: pity.
> Self-pity: the only subject to avoid.

And ends with a kind of invocation of the absent deity:

> One thing is certain. However studious we are, or tough,
> Thank God we cannot hope to know
> The full horror of this world—or whole happiness.
>
> (CP, 22)

In an essay in *Fields of Vision*, 'What happened to the Devil?', Enright is dismissive about modern theology's lack of interest in Evil. He is reviewing Jeffrey Burton Russell's *Lucifer*, and endorses Russell's view that 'at a time when evil threatens to engulf us totally, when evil has already claimed more victims this century than in all previous centuries combined', churchmen evince a lack of interest in the concept.

Russell opines that some modern theologians have been motivated by the thought that the subtraction of Devil / Evil from Christianity would 'remove barriers' and 'be ecumenical'. Yet it is barely credible that theologians could soft-pedal Devil / Evil purely as a tactical, popularizing measure: their personal belief in him / it would surely need to have waned already. (Otherwise, one takes it, they would scarcely leave moral damnation to Chief Constables.) To get rid of God will remove barriers, too, and prove even more ecumenical, for it admits convinced atheists to the Church. Why nibble away at such marginal matters as the Immaculate Conception, the Virgin Birth, the loaves and fishes, the Resurrection? As for the Crucifixion, it was all so very long ago, as they say, that by the grace of God it may not be true.*

And again, in this context, he quotes Mann's *Faustus*, where Leverkühn's 'polymorphous visitor' tells him that only the Devil now speaks of religion: 'Who else, I should like to know, is to speak of it today? Surely not the liberal theologian! After all I am by now its sole custodian! In whom will you recognize theological existence if not in me?' It is as though Enright's interest in, if not need for, religion, arises from the certain existence of the principle of evil, which entails the desire, if never the certainty, for the existence of theological good. In his sequences on *Paradise Lost* and *Faust* he takes on the two most persuasive, elegant, and verbally inventive literary personifications of evil, Milton's spirited sly snake and Goethe's (and Marlowe's) damned and witty Mephistopheles. Both involve evil in the attractions of language and know about damnation. The God in both sequences, by contrast, is a dubious and detached Creator, a kind of poet who uses poetry to evade humanity and the vigorous human (fallen) users of language. It seems necessary to quote the whole of the following poem, since editing it distorts it.

> *Walking in the Harz Mountains,*
> *Faust senses the presence of God*
>
> God was a brooding presence.
> Brooding at present over new metres.
> In which his creatures could approach him,
> In which they could evade him,

* DJE, *Fields of Vision*, 99.

—And he be relieved of their presence,
Through art as Proxy Divine—
Sublimation, as they termed it,
Which could very nearly be sublime—
For which he was truly thankful.

But how active they were, the bad ones!
They brooded rarely.
They talked incessantly,
In poisoned prose from pointed tongues.
How gregarious they were!
They needed friends to wound.

But who had invented tongues?
(One had to be careful when one brooded.)
And even the better ones
(One had to remember)
Were only human . . .
He started to fashion a special measure
For the likes of Gretchen, a still, sad music.

Creation was never finished.

                                        (CP, 241)

This God is weary, reluctant to bother his patrician self (note the use of the reserved 'one', isolating the unique divinity from even the 'better ones' in plural humanity). He is a travesty of the romantic God as artist—his art is a secularized Christ—a 'Proxy Divine'—but its purpose is to distance the creatures. He invents Wordsworth's 'still, sad music of humanity' for the likes of Gretchen, the innocent victims, but his concerns are aesthetic. The last line is splendidly ambiguous. It is God's fatigue with creation. It is the human sense that there is something lacking, something indeed not finished about our raw world. The still, sad music plays, but the devil has all the best tunes. This God as artist is related to an earlier Enright God as poet, working at night, attracting insects to his desk-lamp:

        . . . He gives, He also takes away.

        The insects love the light
        And are devoured. They suppose
        I punish them for something,
        My instrument the spring-jawed dragon.

It isn't difficult to be a god.
You hang your lantern out,
Sink yourself in your own concerns
And leave the rest to the faithful.
                                    ('The Faithful', CP, 101)

Both good and evil, and their myths and religious forms,
are for Enright bound up in the nature of poetry and the
imagination. In the essay on the Devil I've already quoted, he
analyses the myth of Frankenstein's Monster (a kind of unfinished
Adam, requiring love and dignity from his incompetent creator)
and that of Dracula (an embodiment of involuntary, evil
destructiveness) as persisting relics in our culture of 'metaphysical
anxieties':

What this phenomenon, this secret perturbation, has to do with *belief*,
to what extent believing is involved, is hard to say. The postulation of
a half-way house between belief and disbelief is the best we can manage;
that famous 'willing suspension of disbelief for the moment' doesn't fill
the bill, nor does the 'hoping' (or fearing) 'it might be so' of Hardy's
poem, 'The Oxen'. We can agree with William James that what keeps
religion going is 'something else than abstract definitions and systems
of concatenated adjectives, and something different from faculties of
theology and their professors'. And we shall probably find it easier to
assent to Octavio Paz's summing-up: 'Although religions belong to
history and perish, in all of them a non-religious seed survives: poetic
imagination.' Yet the relationship between imagination and belief remains
an indecipherable mystery.*

It is in this context that the project of reworking, in ironic, cross-
referring fragments, the two great myths of Western salvation
and damnation, seems so splendidly ambitious. This essay is
about God, not about language, even though God originated the
tongues in which we damn ourselves so inventively. The poem
in *Sad Ires* on the 'Origin of the Haiku' is a paradigm in little of
the procedures, also in little, but not little, of *Paradise Illustrated*
and *A Faust Book*. It opens Miltonically

                    The darkness is always visible
                    Enough for us to write.

                    * *Fields of Vision*, 110.

goes on to relate all the 'pain' (pains of hell, pains of composition, strictly incomparable?) of making seventeen syllables, relates how a 'desperate faction' proposed to bring in rhyme, and how they were defeated:

> We are a conventional lot,
> This is a conventional spot,
> And we take some satisfaction
> In writing verse called *free*.

It goes on to appropriate, miniaturize, and yet to enliven and continue, the language of Milton's great myth:

> In between we make up epigrams.
> 'Not to know me argues yourselves unknown',
> Or 'What is else not to be overcome?'
> The mind is sometimes its own place.

—this last a splendidly ironic statement, since its space is two quotations from God and Satan respectively, and its (original) context is lack of freedom.

> Such petty projects—
> Yes, but even an epic,
> Even *Paradise Lost*,
> Would look puny
> In hell, throughout eternity . . .
>
> (CP, 157–8)

Space, time, eternity, poetry, heaven and hell, and a technical exercise, all connected. An equal sense of crafted proportion and huge disproportion. Language, including Milton's, saves. Language does nothing at all about the fact that Enright keeps echoing and half-echoing, 'Why, this is Hell, / And we are in it.' Or 'Y this is L / Nor-my-outfit.'

The Paradise myth, Enright claimed, although it had been criticized for not holding any enduring truth, did, on the contrary,

engage readers (in diverse Asian countries, for example) who are not Christian either by conviction or, laxly, by environment. For it is the story of our first parents, of the birth of moral consciousness, and pre-eminently of the perversity in human nature whereby man destroys his happiness even when outward circumstance works in its favour and to his benefit. The Christian myth in some of its elements exerts a greater persisting influence on—or is more actively central to—not only our ethics (increasingly international) but also the darker places of the human psyche than is often supposed, even (or especially) by its conscious adherents.*

Enright incarnates this myth, in accounts farcical, grim, joky, of our incorrigible sinfulness. I like particularly, in this context, his picture of himself teaching Hopkins in the Orient ('More Memories of Underdevelopment'):

> 'God's most deep decree
> Bitter would have me taste: my taste was me.'

The poet describes himself as a 'lapsed Wesleyan' (lapsed again) who is teaching Father Hopkins to 'these young though ageless Catholics'. He asks

> A lurching humanist,
> Is it for me to instruct you in the fall complete?

He himself is ironically moved by Hopkins's words:

> Yet these words appal me with recognition,
> They grow continuously in terror.

Yet his innocent charges assume that his response is due to his age:

> Oh yes, they tell themselves, the poor old man,
> His taste is certainly him . . .
> And they turn to their nicer thoughts,
> Of salted mangoes, pickled plums, and bamboo shoots,
> And scarlet chillies, and rice as white as snow.
>
> (CP, 103)

Their image of themselves is an unfallen paradise, yet it contains a hint of Christian iconography in the last line—though their sins are as scarlet, yet they shall be washed whiter than snow—which is ambiguous, if read one way. Either in this land Christian myths are without force, and scarlet and white tastes are nothing to do with original sin. Or the sin lurks in the innocent taste, as it does in the flowery crown of Marvell's Little T.C., for instance. Either way the contrast between the lapsed humanist with his powerful sense of innate evil and the colourfully wholesome young is piquant.

---

* *A Choice of Milton's Verse*, 11.

Such ambiguous resonances have been the stuff of religious poetry through the centuries. I want finally to consider a peculiar kind of Christian presence in Enright's presentation of ordinary language and culture in our demythologized world. In *Paradise Illustrated*, language is the naming of things, pre- and post-lapsarian, flowers and creatures before the Fall—'Avalanches, defoliation, earthquakes, eruptions . . . Also perhaps inclemency', as Adam remarks in a fit of 'airy' inventiveness (XIII). In the *Faust Book* language is romantic, as we have seen in the Harz Mountains, or may see in Mephistopheles's argument with the simple primrose. In *Paradise Illustrated* (XIX) Raphael tells Adam that a long book will be written about this very matter, and suggests that the real hero is the Son.

In Section XVIII God and the Son have a dialogue:

> '*My sole complacence,*
> *Radiant image of My Glory!*'
>
> 'What I mean precisely.
> Much further, Father. You must love—
> And love what's hard to love.'
>
> '*Too much talk of love.*
> *Die man, or someone else must die.*'
>
> 'Account me man *pro tem*.
> *Pro tem* account me man.'
>
> Nothing was said about a cross.
> By now the quire was in full swing.
>   (CP, 187)

I think it is not fanciful to see in the accountant's language, *pro tem*, a version of the Incarnation in the vulgar and mundane—and temporal. In the context of the reduced epic, the language has its Herbertian riddling ambiguity. But in our world, as Enright shows, the myths can be strangely inert, can bristle with oddity and a kind of questionable vampiric life.

There is, again, a childish or innocent version of what I mean in *The Terrible Shears*, in which secular things acquire the moral and emotive power of the sacred ones, even challenge them, as when the poet reflects on the worse fate of women ('Religious Phase'):

> He was on secondment. At no time
> Was he ignorant of his state.
>
> His ignorant bewildered mother
> Was another matter.
> In our street the pangs of labour
> Were nearer than those of crucifixion.
> Carpenters were useful, but
> Every family required a mother.
>   (CP, 149–50)

This draws its strength from its plainness and its relation to what we are told about the poet's mother. More ambivalent in its tone is one of the little poems about Christmas:

> The cracked oilcloth is hidden
> By knife-creased linen.
> On it bottles of Vimto squat,
> A few flakes of browning tinsel
> Settle. It is Christmas—
> Someone will pay for this.
>   (CP, 123)

'Someone will pay' is the sober truth, and the ironic reference to the atonement that follows the celebration of the birth. Here again the once powerful meanings of the phrases haunt the solid and daily. Something similar is happening in the poem 'Remembrance Sunday', from *Sad Ires*:

> The autumn leaves that strew the brooks
> Lie thick as legions.
>   Only a dog limps past,
> Lifting a wounded leg.
>   Was it the rocket hurt it?
> Asks a child.
>   And next comes Xmas,
> Reflects the mother in the silence,
> When X was born or hurt or died.
>   (CP, 173)

This is beautiful and complex, in its contrast of the Miltonic and Dantesque fallen soldiers with the blunt ciphered absence of X, to whom it is all one, whether he was born or hurt or died—he is humanized by the word 'hurt' which carries pain and power.

Between Milton and X are a dog (a limp and wounded God?—
see the *Faust Book* on dogs and poodles) and a child, concerned
with rockets. But this poem too evokes what has gone from our
culture, X.

The 'feel' of the presence and absence of Christ is different in
a poem like 'The Stations of King's Cross', which is bizarrely
witty, straining for effect, a kind of modern Gongorism. It finds
the Passion in ordinary language with fiendish ingenuity.

> At Hammersmith the nails
> At Green Park the tree.
>
> .   .   .   .   .
>
> He speaks to the maidenforms of Jerusalem
> Blessed are the paps which never gave suck.
>
> .   .   .   .   .
>
> The first fall, the second fall
> The third fall.
> And more to come.
>
> A sleeve goes, a leg is torn
> A hem is ripped.
> This is the parting of garments.
>
> They mock him, offering him vodka.
> The effect is shattering.
>
> He is taken down from the strap.
> And deposited.
>
> Wilt thou leave him in the loathsome grave?
>   (CP, 156–7)

What sort of poem is this? Why describe the hazards of modern
tube-travel in terms of the ancient and once-believed-in journey
of the god-man to torture and death? It is not, as we have seen,
that Enright takes pleasure in iconoclasm, nor is it any kind of
fashionable sick wit. What I think it is is a showing-up of the
vanishing of what was the centre of our public culture and private
myths. Only those of us who know these myths or stories will
pick up the system of connections at work. If we do, we will be
made uncomfortably aware of the absence from much public life
now of any interest in, or ability to make, such connections. Why
this is hell nor are we out of it, might indeed be jocularly said

of strap-hanging, but this Hell will not be harrowed, and if there is no Man to speak for the strap-hanger, his small concerns will remain small. The language, however, always for those of us who can read it, has acquired a new and savage vitality, almost demonic?

Some of Enright's very recent poems have made me laugh aloud, almost hysterically, partly because they were verbally funny, but partly because they called up obscure emotions I feel, as a resolute anti-Christian, about the vanishing of the whole culture, the whole spread of heaven, hell, and suffering meaning I grew up with. Such poems, or proses, are 'Agape', 'Psalm for Supersunday' and 'Prayer'.

'Agape' is about the question of whether God struck York Minster because of the consecration of the Bishop of Durham. It rollicks. It is rather naughty, or wicked, in its suggestion that the old God might after all act in a traditional manner and smite those he was displeased with. But its language is couched in a mad debating form that leaves no opening for such a vision:

> question: Why did God not strike Durham Cathedral? Is it suggested that His aim is uncertain?
>
> answer: In His mysterious way He reveals that He moves in a mysterious way.
>
> question: Though less mysterious, would it not have been more to the point to strike down Arthur Scargill?
>
> rebuke: The Archbishop of Canterbury does not care for talk of divine intervention unless properly vouched for.
>
> (CP, 353)

What is the effect of this? Some people laugh a great deal when I show it to them; some look pained, at bad taste or triviality. I myself believe that the poem *is* a light-hearted but devastating attack on the deadness of modern religion, on the lifelessness acknowledged by Leverkühn's lively visitor. God does not strike any longer. When he appears to, we know it is not him, because we know he is not there (as the Bishop of Durham probably knows also.) What religion we have has no poetic or other vitality. To spell this out is to do the poem a disservice. It works in contrast to the God we all learned about in school, in hours of boredom and flashes of sublimity and vision. It proclaims his absence and ineffectiveness. His mysterious ways are merely a tautology.

'Psalm for Supersunday' is naturalized religion with a vengeance—or not, since it is all safe and sanitized? The supermarket is sanitized, but not Enright's demonic language. This psalm addresses the entropic final vision of the Sunday 'brisk person' of *The Terrible Shears*, and it presents simultaneously the resolutely unheard cry of this person's Proxy Divine, the incarnate, the ruthlessly demythologized and annihilated Christ:

> There on the right you shall find bread, white and brown, sliced and unsliced; and on the left new wine in new bottles, made to make men glad. Vinegar is displayed elsewhere and, in Toiletries, sponges.
> This was somebody's flesh and blood, they say, speaking metaphorically. The Supermarket, as likewise the lesser clergy, has set its face against metaphors, save in promotional literature. The beef is immaculately presented, not conceived; the lamb will never rise again.
>
> (CP, 354)

This is demythologized and desacralized. Bread and wine, vinegar and sponge, are stripped of their associations. The mention of metaphor is peculiarly interesting, because it is detached from any context of meaning. 'They say' this was 'somebody's flesh and blood', where 'they' is vanishing, gossipy, and vague—who say?—and 'someone' is more pallid, amorphous, and ineffective than the X of the earlier poem in which he was born or hurt or died. The vanishing of our contexts and meanings is enacted at us, but because we can still pick up these inert references and remember the power that was in them, they are a form of torment for us. I think the absence of metaphor is more unpleasant than the commercial world of the Sunday Supermarket; to my ear the final secular joke about the cash registers—'Hearken to the sound of bells'—is funnier, perhaps because the joke about money as an alternative God is old, whereas the absence of metaphor and myth is not. Though one remembers, as perhaps was appropriate in the earlier context of the Sunday flowers in which the poet would now 'see' only 'the sound of Sunday church bells', one of George Herbert's lovely, multifarious metaphors for prayer, uniting Heaven and earth, 'Church bells beyond the stars heard'. Enright's absent God at his best and most desired is most often Herbert's God, whose voice, Christ's voice, Enright's Faust hears in parenthesis, signing his demonic contract:

(Some other words were heard in Faustus' mind.
There is in love a sweetnesse readie penn'd:
Copie out onely that, and save expense—
But reason could not tell him what they meant.)

Which brings me to a final poem, appropriately entitled
'Prayer'. This again looks like a squib, a verbal *tour de force*, a kind
of wicked game with the respectably sacred. But it is not finally
that, though it depends upon arbitrary puns (sin / sun / cindy /
Sunday) for part of its effect. Much of what I have been looking
at in this essay is given a new shape here, at once grisly and
gentle, bereft of significance and full of pain, immersed in the
world of post-Sunday *pro tem* accountancy. It is awfully funny.
Like the world, according to Enright.

O Cindy
You who are always well-groomed and cheerful
As we should be
Who tie your hair back before going to ballet school
As we should do
Who take good care of your costly vestments
As we should take
Who is put to bed and made to get up
Who speak in silent parables
Concerning charm and deportment and a suitable marriage
   to a tennis star and yachts and a rich social life
Who grow old like us
Yet unlike us remain for ever young
Whose hair is torn out at times
Whose arms are broken
Whose legs are forced apart
Who take away the sin of the world
To whom a raggedy doll called Barabbas is preferred
You who are scourged
And given vinegar to drink from a jar of pickled onions
Who seem to say, Why have you forsaken me?
Who like us may rise or may not from the dead
   in a long white garment
You after whom the first day of the week is almost named
Into your hands we commend ourselves.

                                               (CP, 355)

Untold Stories

SHIRLEY CHEW

IN an uncollected sequence by D. J. Enright, called 'Scenes of
Literary Life', this verse occurs:

> The *Lust zu fabulieren*!—Throw oneself
> Upon the body of this life. A rage to recreate,
> To crystallize the *donna mobile*. To rape
> A tempting senselessness. To know oneself.
>
> ('Story-Teller')

—where *Lust zu fabulieren* (from a poem of Goethe's, 'Den
Originalen') means 'joy in telling stories', the word *Lust* combining
'pleasure' with suggestions of 'longing' and even 'lust'. In
Enright, this desire (stated here with unusual violence) to find
stability in mutability, to make sense out of senselessness, to
know, has its origins in the experience of growing up in the
England of the 1920s and 1930s, as his sequence *The Terrible Shears*
(1973) makes clear. One critical moment of arrival at knowledge
is the subject of a much earlier poem, 'First Death'.

> It is terrible and wonderful: we wake in the strange night
> And there is one bed empty and one room full: tears fall,
> The children comfort each other, hugging their knees,
>   for what will the future be now, poor things?
>
> And next day there is no school, and meals are disorderly,
> Things bought from shops, not the old familiar dishes.
> New uncles come from far away, soft-voiced strangers
> Drinking extraordinary wines. A kind of abstract kindliness
> Fills the house, and a smell of flowers. Impossible to be bad—
>
> Other nights pass, under conceded night-lights and a cloud
> Of questions: shall we ever go back to school? Ever again
> Go to the pictures? Are we too poor for new shoes?
>   Must we move
> To a council house? Will any of our friends remember us?
> Will it always be kind and quiet and sad, like this?

Uncles depart. We go for a week to a country aunt,
Then take a lodger. New shoes are bought—Oh,
   so this is the future!
How long will it last, this time? Never feel safe now.

                    (CP, 4)

The success of 'First Death' is due in part to the simple but firm lines of its structure within which a situation full of exciting as well as worrying possibilities ends in betrayal; in part to the play of different registers of language—lyrical, colloquial, formal, interjectory—that catches so delicately the quick shifts of the children's consciousness. As the story moves from a state of disruption to the recovery signalled in the last stanza, so it is clear that knowledge of some kind has been gained. But while an extractable lesson ends the poem, 'Never feel safe now', the specific nature of the knowledge which lies behind it is left undisclosed. Perhaps William Walsh is right to read this 'terrified realization' into the silence: 'the future is no simple flowering of a fragrant present, but the intrusion into [the children's] lives of a dangerous, treacherous force.'* Alternatively it may be that what is realized is the unchanging nature of change— new shoes are bought after all; and that whatever change there is can only be for the worse—there is a lodger. Whichever the interpretation, the point is that no neat correspondence exists between story and lesson here as in, say, Philip Larkin's 'I Remember, I Remember', nor does the poem, as it has been said of 'Dockery & Son', gather 'to a conclusion of great impact'.** A narrative that sets out to 'make sense', 'First Death' proceeds instead to call narrative codes into question and retreats into concealment when the crisis-point is reached, as if acknowledging the impossibility of its task.

All the same, to note the preponderance of stories and their variety in *Collected Poems 1987* is to be left in no doubt that the *Lust zu fabulieren* in Enright's case was whetted by his experience abroad. Largely, the 'joy' in the narratives about Egypt, Japan, Thailand, and Singapore lies in discovering a way through the simply unfamiliar or the calculatedly exotic to the 'common thing'

---

* D. J. Enright: Poet of Humanism, CUP, 1974, 32.
  ** Barbara Everett, 'Larkin and Dockery: the Limits of the Social', in *Philip Larkin 1922–1985: A Tribute*, ed. George Hartley, Marvell Press, 1988, 146.

and 'human idiom' beyond. Past the Zen garden, there are 'life-size people, / Rooted in precious little'; in the opium den in Bangkok, the poor clutch their 'banks of dreams'; among the patrons of the Shanghai restaurant in Singapore is one elderly Chinese gentleman whom 'it would be agreeable to be'. Moments of 'knowing', such as these, are clearly important to Enright. Nevertheless, the ambiguities of the story-teller's art persist as a problem of ongoing concern in his poetry. On the one hand, 'To tell a story is to find a way—sometimes the only way—of *knowing* one's world'.* On the other, the world does not necessarily make sense, as 'First Death' has indicated, and driven by the desire to *know* in the face of resistance, the story-teller is liable to find himself imposing meaning as much as seeking it.

'In the Catalogue' enacts the dilemma, narrating an encounter in Japan one night with a featureless 'figure' swathed in straw, and the efforts made to bring the 'thing' within the pale of the recognizable and the human. A sort of traveller's tale, the poem uncovers the panic which, however well-hidden, forms part of the psychological baggage of the visitor to strange lands—'It was a foreign horror'. At the same time, 'foreign' meaning 'situated outside the bounds of the human', this traveller's tale of the 1950s tilts at the limits of humanism, 'a good idea since ruined', and moreover an idea informing Enright's own writing. *Homo sum; humani nil a me alienum puto*—the only risk is that what constitutes 'human' is likely to be self-referential.

To follow Macbeth's speech directed at the men employed to kill Banquo, and from which the phrase 'in the catalogue' is taken, is to arrive at the ironical conclusion that one must turn murderer in order to prove a 'man' (human as well as manly). In Enright's poem, a corresponding situation occurs in which the narrator's status as 'man' depends upon his ability to humanize the 'foreign horror' and convert it into a familiar tourist sight, such as a cherry sapling or a beggar. His actions—braving the unknown, proffering charity, expressing fear and anger, keeping down his stomach—appear to have no value until distance and poor light, coming to his aid, cast up an image which allows him to view

---

* Marjorie Perloff, *The Dance of the Intellect: Studies in the poetry of the Pound tradition*, CUP, 1985, 161.

the incomprehensible in relation to himself and thereby to
translate the entire incident into meaning.

> From twenty yards I turned
> To look. The shape stood still.
> Another ten yards, and I strained
> My eyes on icy shadows—
>
> The shape was scrabbling for my coins!
> I thanked my stomach. Then
> Thanked God, who'd left the thing
> Enough to make a man.
>
> (CP, 66-7)

Relief and strong assertion bring the narrator's tale to a close.
Meanwhile, unyielding in its silence, the 'foreign horror'
continues to elude definition.

Some thirty years later, uncertainties can only multiply when,
in his various roles of visiting poet, foreigner, tourist, Enright is
taken sightseeing in China. 'An Old Story' recounts the fate of
the legendary sculptor who, having completed only 999 of the
emperor's thousand Buddhas when the deadline arrived, resorted
to posing as the unfinished item of art in a desperate attempt to
save his head. Very likely the ruse would not have worked but,
as it was, 'some benign and witty divinity' intervened, turning
him into stone. Not that he evaded the executioner entirely for,
years later during the Cultural Revolution, the thousand Buddhas,
along with other cultural objects, fell into disgrace and thus victim
to the sledge-hammers.

> See, he has lost his head. But otherwise he is all there.
> Which can hardly be said of some of us standing here,
> Encouraged to gawk, now that policies have been slightly reversed
> And the past is permitted. And we mutter ruefully an apt
> And innocuous proverb: 'Easier to pull down than to build up',
> Cocking our heads, unsure what to do with our hands.
>
> (CP, 343-4)

Mixing legend and history, fact and fiction, the serious and the
comic, instruction and entertainment, 'An Old Story' is cleverly
constructed and possesses the 'very specific syntactic shape
(beginning–middle–end or situation–transformation–situation)'
which, according to Robert Scholes, differentiates story, a more

'rule-governed' category, from narrative.* At the same time, the
verse moves with ease and point, an appropriate vehicle for the
practised raconteur with a zest for the concrete and the skill to
make the details telling. Like all good stories, this one has a lesson
to teach: 'Easier to pull down than build up.' Like the best of
them, its meaning exceeds the limits of this 'apt and innocuous
proverb', and hovers, moreover, where the statements do not
quite fit, the interstices of language.

The seeming absurdity (two contradictions in the single
statement) of 'See, he has lost his head [without his wits about
him]. But otherwise he is all there [has his wits about him]',
is readily spotted by the narrator, speaking on behalf of the other
foreign visitors. This gobbledegook intensifies his disquiet,
demonstrating that whichever way the pendulum swings—
whether China is imperial or Communist and whether Buddhas
are in or out of favour—it is the unchanging rule that ordinary
people without much power have the most to lose. An ordinary
person himself and a poet, it is natural that the narrator should
feel for the ancient sculptor, so that 'heads' and 'hands', the
aesthetic features of all Buddhas, become the projections also of
his individual unease and a reminder of his vulnerability.

But the story-teller's voice is not the only one to be heard in
this poem. Though a fleeting intrusion, there is another voice
which asks to be properly transcribed. 'See, [the statue] has lost
[its] head. But [in other respects] [it] is unimpaired.' With its
sense restored, the statement is open to interpretations other than
the one put forward by the narrator. It offers a reading of the
damaged Buddha which intimates the tenacity of ordinary people
who have to make do and survive, however piecemeal, the
dictates of powerful rulers and regimes, and who must believe
that a kind of extrication is possible. The difference underlined
is between 'seeing' and 'gawking', between an insider's
perspective of the broad historical canvas made available in this
story and an outsider's. Though even the gifts of the gods, it has
to be borne in mind, are mixed blessings: 'See, he has [failed
to keep his wits about him]. But [in another fashion, if not quite
in the way he expected] he is [materially intact].' 'What better

* 'Language, Narrative, and Anti-Narrative', *Critical Inquiry*, 7 (Autumn, 1980),
210.

check on general doctrine can there be than the poet's or the novelist's "small stories", told with verve and generosity?' asks Enright.* And what better safeguard against the poet's and the novelist's *Lust* to impose their own ways of knowing than these same 'small stories'?

If 'An Old Story', compared to the earlier 'In the Catalogue', strikes one as possessing a greater flexibility, enabling it to bring together several narrative modes and voices, this may be attributed to Enright's increasing experience in working with verse sequences. 'For their authors, at any rate, verse sequences hold a particular charm—they combine the pleasures of writing poetry with the pleasure of telling a story (and, one might add, without the pains imposed on the novelist by the necessity for continuity and explanation).'** In that statement, Enright identifies one of the reasons for the success of *A Faust Book* (1979)—the commodiousness of its form. Another rests with the versatility of the Faust story itself as a vehicle of the human desire to know and the limits of knowledge. Form and subject-matter agreeing, it is not surprising that Enright's retelling of the legend should delight with its wit, fertile invention, and gravity wedded to a buoyant sense of the comic.

In the last poem of the sequence, 'Faust and Mephistopheles make their adieus', the bond is cancelled and the two characters pause to count their losses before going their separate ways:

> 'You'll miss me, Faust. I was your muse.
> Who will amuse you now?'

> The one considered things to do in time.
> The other thought of things that time could do.
> The stars stood still, the clock marked time.

> 'That's true, my friend,' Faust sighed.
> You've ruined me for other company.
> I'll pass my days in some far wilderness.'

---

* 'More than Mere Biology', in *Fields of Vision: Essays on Literature, Language, and Television*, OUP, 1988, 171.
** *The Poetry Book Society Bulletin*, 102 (Autumn, 1979).

Was there no wilderness at hand?
'I'll miss you too,' said Mephistopheles.
'But then, I'm used to missing . . .'
                                    (CP, 263)

As a recreation of the legendary hero, Enright's Faust, a
dissatisfied university don, cannot be said to be overly sensitive
or aspiring. For one who has kept company with the Devil
for twelve years (the contracted span of time cleverly cut
down by Mephistopheles) and narrowly escaped damnation, he
stays even at the end curiously bound to the dictates of
his senses ('how his hand had hurt'), to temporality ('things
to do in time'), and a literal notion of space ('some far
wilderness'). It seems proper, therefore, that in this version of
the story his more dazzling companion should have the last
word, and particularly as Mephistopheles suspects he has
been let down by his own side and got the worst of the bargain.
The result is to frustrate the reader's desire for closure and
also to turn attention back to some of the most compelling
moments of the poem. 'But then, I'm used to missing . . .' A
simple turn of speech, its power to move springs from the
cumulative technique of the form which enables repetition
with difference and a concentration on the parts with a
progressive sense of the whole. To read items such as 'Faust
grows impatient with his companion's dark mutterings', 'Faust
requires Mephistopheles to describe hell and heaven for him',
'Mephistopheles is sorely embarrassed', is to be drawn into a
complicated word-game made up of puns, jokes, allusions, in
which linguistic puzzles serve to underpin serious issues. If hell
is the opposite of heaven and its liturgies 'run widdershins', if
hell is for Mephistopheles all too present and heaven entirely
absent, if Mephistopheles finds it hard 'to comprehend his
master' and lacks authority to comprehend God, then the way
to proceed when catechized by Faust on hell and heaven is by
indirection, satisfied to speak in riddles, to find the part that
stands for the whole, the epithets that stand counter. These
strategies say much about the nature of language and about the
nature of desire. At the same time, they reflect Mephistopheles's
many-sidedness—duplicity, urbanity, pragmatism, remorseless-
ness, cynicism—and his tragic knowledge of loss.

There is irony, in that on the occasions when Mephistopheles's control slips, as in 'Mephistopheles remembers the face of God', and the eternal yearning which is his hell is exposed, nobody is really paying attention:

> 'Do you suppose that I
> Who used to look upon the naked face of God
> Would not do anything
> To look again?
>
> Should a ladder stretch to heaven,
> Its rungs all razor blades
> That slice me to the loins
> At every step—
> Yet I would do my best
> To climb that endless edge,
>
> To look once more,
> Then backwards fall
> To timelessness in hell.

(CP, 227-8)

Such opportunity for knowing again is, of course, denied him and the hopelessness—carried in the reach and retraction of the verse, the hollow notes of 'more', 'fall', 'hell'—has the power to move. Unfortunately, Faust is too busy seeking physical satisfactions at this point to stop to listen.

It may be said of Enright that he has had, like Mephistopheles, 'his wits sharpened by experience of several worlds'.* In which case, what could be more natural than to remake himself as the main character in his next verse sequence, *Instant Chronicles: A Life* (1985). Bearing in mind the lengths to which some modern biographies are prepared to go, Enright has elsewhere described the form as tending towards 'a highly dubious enterprise. Its author is concerned with, concerned to re-create, another person, a real (even if dead) one, of whom he is bound to know less than all and whom, with insufficient sure evidence to go on, he is bound to keep judging whether or not he intends or desires to.'**

---

* *The Poetry Book Society Bulletin*, 102 (Autumn, 1979).
** 'Democracy of Gods: a Life of Heine', in *A Mania for Sentences*, Chatto & Windus, 1983, 3.

Instant Chronicles is in one reading a take-off of this sort of enterprise, for it is Enright who opens this sequence of poems and prose items, invents the lively headings, many of which would not be out of place in a novel, and pursues himself across the world and through his own papers. The joke is at the biographer's expense, however, since what comes to light in the course of the hunt are non-discoveries ('Secret drawer'), or nonsense ('Naming names'), or inconclusive evidence ('Love poem').

Much is deliberately concealed or simply ignored in *Instant Chronicles* but, if one 'life' does not get written, another does, for the sequence as a whole, and in its parts, grows out of a principle of closures and expansions, loss and recovery. The biographer is only one of the multiple roles which Enright adopts, and one which may be merged with, or undercut, or displaced by, his other roles as poet, autobiographer, travel-writer, historian. In 'Explanations', for example, two voices appear to be jostling for authority, complicated at times by the intrusion of the voice of 'his folk'. To the biographer, the poet's background clearly accounts for his leanings as a writer. Considering its inhibiting narrowness,

> No wonder that foreigners, the most outlandish,
> Were the only subject he felt at home with—
> As if they'd want a literature, and one in English!
>   (CP, 288)

Against the plainness of this interpretation, the swing of the verse, away towards 'outlandish' only to come back to 'at home with', suggests that somewhere between the two extremes of 'his folk' and 'foreigners', between those 'excessively averse to exaggeration' and those excessively given to it, there is a measure of common ground, the exact location of which has to be continually staked out by the imagination.

This idea is enacted repeatedly in the sequence and with especial exuberance in an extended image of collaborative fiction-making in the prose item 'At the theatre'. Here the writing recreates that experience peculiar to *Kabuki* theatre which is (or used to be) a combined affair of dramatic performance and audience participation. 'An actor freezes into an extravagant pose, a stylized grimace. ''That's it!'' they shout. ''That's what we've been waiting for!'' They know a famous moment when they see one.' The plot of the play depends on various kinds of deception, since it is by means of disguises, misleading words and deeds, that the truth can be simultaneously concealed and revealed, and emotion be pleasurably concentrated.

What agony for Benkei to strike his Lord! What agony for Togashi to watch Benkei striking his Lord! What delicious anguish for the audience to witness Togashi suffering for Benkei, Benkei suffering for his Lord, and his Lord suffering! Men of honour, all.

Despite Enright's sly humour at this open enjoyment of feeling, he too can tell an outstanding moment when he sees one:

Wooden clappers signal the climax. (And wake a baby up: out comes an absent-minded breast.) To the sound of a drum, Benkei begins his triumphant exit, along the 'flower way' through the audience, taking his time, in ecstatic monstrous hops. An old man calls out the actor's name: 'You're every bit as good as your father was!'

(CP, 297–8)

His prose conducts itself like an expert, bringing about through its movement and ordering the splendid coincidence of English language, foreign culture, fiction, history, actor, audience, art, and life.

The years have brought changes, inevitably, and with these, different ways of seeing and knowing. The incident in Bangkok that was treated at some length in the novel *Figures of Speech* (1965) and *Memoirs of a Mendicant Professor* (1969) survives here in a poem of eight lines.

Roughed up by a dozen tipsy and excited policemen,
He found solace in sensing, between buffets, certain
Gradations of violence, even faint reluctances
(For whatever reason), and a pulling of punches.
He was comforted to note, between unfatal kicks,
A gun drawn but knocked by someone to the pavement.
All this arose from a pure and simple misjudgement—
In a time between Terrors, nothing to do with politics.

('Pure Accident', CP, 302)

Poet and biographer seem to agree upon deflecting attention from the painful feelings suffered on that occasion and the ironies are well-gauged. Just as the blows did not carry their full impact, so 'pure accident', 'roughed up', 'a pulling of punches' are commonplaces all; and while 'pavement' rhyming with 'misjudgement' brings the separate versions of the story, the personal and the official, to a close, the last line retrieves the incident as a sign of the times ('nothing to do with politics' harks back after all to 'unfatal kicks').

Not every aspect of the past however lends itself to the clarity of redefinition. The basis of Enright's quarrel in Singapore with the PAP government can now be established, as in 'In hot water'. But it is still difficult to pin down his feelings relating to the event, a difficulty exacerbated perhaps by the recognition that he was in this instance not altogether the innocent victim of an accident. Where there are no easy answers, an amount of nimble circling and tacking about has to be done, and some of the reflections on Singapore involve a search for a point of view other than his own or that of those in power.

> An odd sensation, to enter a favourite bar
> And hear oneself denounced on the radio.
>
> (A change from queuing in some homely pub
> To buy a pint, inaudible, ignored.)
>
> The waiters were incurious. They had heard
> So many scoldings, in so many tongues.
>
> Moon-faced and beaming, to and fro they slid
> With trays of drinks, not a drop slopped over—
>
> Knowing that music was soon to follow,
> Noble and wicked sentiments from Chinese opera.
> ('Interrupting the programme', CP, 305)

Agile like the waiters' performance, the verse moves away from the personal predicament in order to come back to it from the perspective of ordinary people, who wish to be neither heroes nor villains, and fear they are liable to be victims.

Enright identifies with these non-heroes (and in other guises they have a voice and a place in this work as elsewhere in his poetry) but as an expatriate he is also distanced from them. In many instances, the feeling of attachment is conveyed paradoxically in images of withdrawal, until in 'Home' the figure of the poet is missing altogether, and only fragments of local history remain to suggest a kind of presence—an old house, the Japanese occupying army, the invading monkeys from the nearby Botanic Gardens, and a post-imperial Englishman whose name transliterated into Japanese reads 'Monkey comes to town'.

On the subject of growing old, clearly the biographer must give place to the ageing poet. The power of the writing in the last items of the sequence springs in part from the cohesiveness of the narrative for here, as previously, are the motifs of moving on, impending disaster, and powerlessness. But instead of tipsy policemen, ominous forces are at work, and instead of earthly dictators, there is a doubtful sort of God so that, familiar in some ways though the predicament may be, it is in others new and fascinating to the imagination. The steady encroachments upon the flesh and spirit—'lawless pangs and migrant uneases'—are wittily and poignantly observed and there is an infusion of energy as the narrator manœuvres compulsively between the awfulness of the situation and a disinterested even comic view of it. Among his strategies are those of obliqueness ('Where can it be?' purports to search for the soul across the depressing landscape of a worn-out body), studied juxtaposition ('Instruments to plague' sets the gathering symptoms of 'failing sight, strange warts and gout' against the sudden and undeserved fate of 'those, the utterly / Innocent, struck down already, finally'), and indeterminacy ('The evil days', in parodying Ecclesiastes 12, blends and blurs the poetic and the mundane, the irreverent and the lofty). Until the very end, 'Last things', the mind paces restlessly among the possibilities which are open to it, its checks and starts sensitively enacted by the verse. But because it is not really deceived about the situation, it can only proceed upon a series of conditionals and qualified negatives towards what is in fact the absence of choice: 'At least go in peace, since you must go, in peace.'

The final and darkest passage in the sequence, 'Ever-rolling', recapitulates the theme of emotional and spiritual attrition in a world whose attempts to remake itself have resulted in unending and 'undistinguished horrors'. As always in Enright's poetry, the thought, the language, the curves and angles of the voice find each other out, and here the burden of despair is impressively carried by the verse, eloquent, resonant, and propelled towards answers and solutions not forthcoming.

If all the innocents, the slaughtered commons,
Swollen children, if only they could rise

In one great cloud to heaven, at least
The guiltless, could go and leave us free,

Leave us a yet unwritten page. A virgin year,
And this tired soil lie fallow. What might follow?

We thought we prized the past, its noble gifts,
White elephants that ate us out of heart and home.

If on the moon mankind could lose its memories;
On some fiery star our brains be wiped quite clean.

Until which time we make our unfresh starts
And share our instant chronicles. It's your turn now.
                    (CP, 339–40)

In the end the only certainties are the small resources we already possess. But 'unfresh starts' and 'instant chronicles' need not be such bad things since, as Enright has so persuasively demonstrated, out of them can come new ways of knowing.

SELECT BIBLIOGRAPHY

References in the book are to the page numbers of the paperback
Collected Poems 1987

POETRY

Season Ticket, Aux Editions du Scarabée, Alexandria, 1948.
The Laughing Hyena and Other Poems, Routledge and Kegan Paul, 1953.
Bread Rather than Blossoms, Secker and Warburg, 1956.
Some Men Are Brothers, Chatto & Windus, 1960.
Addictions, Chatto & Windus, 1962.
The Old Adam, Chatto & Windus, 1965.
Selected Poems, Chatto & Windus, 1968.
The Typewriter Revolution and Other Poems, Library Press, New York, 1971.
Unlawful Assembly, Chatto & Windus, 1968.
Daughters of Earth, Chatto & Windus, 1972.
Foreign Devils, Covent Garden Press, 1972.
The Terrible Shears: Scenes from a Twenties Childhood, Chatto & Windus,
    1973; Wesleyan University Press, 1974.
Rhyme Times Rhyme (juvenile), Chatto & Windus, 1974.
Sad Ires, Chatto & Windus, 1975.
Penguin Modern Poets, 26: Dannie Abse, D. J. Enright, Michael Longley,
    Penguin, 1975.
Paradise Illustrated, Chatto & Windus, 1978.
A Faust Book, OUP, Oxford and New York, 1979.
Collected Poems, OUP, 1981 (with new poems).
Instant Chronicles, A Life, OUP, 1985.
Collected Poems 1987 (enlarged edition), OUP, 1987 (including *Instant
    Chronicles*, additional poems, and new poems); paperback (Oxford
    Poets).
Selected Poems 1990 [from *Collected Poems 1987*], OUP, 1990, paperback
    (Oxford Poets).

NOVELS

Academic Year, Secker & Warburg, 1955; repr. Buchan & Enright, 1984;
    OUP (Twentieth-Century Classics) 1985.
Heaven Knows Where, Secker & Warburg, 1957.
Insufficient Poppy, Chatto & Windus, 1960.
Figures of Speech, Heinemann, 1965.
The Joke Shop (juvenile), Chatto & Windus, 1976; David McKay Co., New
    York.

Wild Ghost Chase (juvenile), Chatto & Windus, 1978.
Beyond Land's End (juvenile), Chatto & Windus, 1979.

ESSAYS

Literature for Man's Sake, Kenkyusha, Tokyo, 1955; repr. Richard West, 1976.
The Apothecary's Shop: Essays on Literature, Secker & Warburg, 1957; Dufour, 1959; repr. Greenwood Press, 1975.
Conspirators and Poets, Chatto & Windus, 1966; Dufour, 1966.
Man Is an Onion: Reviews and Essays, Chatto & Windus, 1972; Library Press, 1973.
A Mania for Sentences, Chatto & Windus, 1983; Godine, 1985.
The Alluring Problem, An Essay on Irony, OUP, 1986.
Fields of Vision, Essays on Literature, Language, and Television, OUP, 1988.

WRITINGS

A Commentary on Goethe's 'Faust', New Directions, 1949.
The World of Dew: Aspects of Living Japan, Secker & Warburg, 1955.
Robert Graves and the Decline of Modernism, lecture, Craftsman Press, Singapore, 1960. (Repr. in *Conspirators and Poets*, see above.)
Memoirs of a Mendicant Professor (autobiography), Chatto & Windus, 1969; repr. Carcanet Press, 1990.
Shakespeare and the Students, Chatto & Windus, 1970; Schocken, 1971.

EDITIONS AND ANTHOLOGIES

Poetry of the 1950's: An Anthology of New English Verse, Kenkyusha, Tokyo, 1955.
The Poetry of Living Japan (with Takamichi Ninomiya), John Murray, Grove, 1957.
English Critical Texts. 16th Century to 20th Century (with Ernst de Chickera). OUP, 1962.
John Milton, *A Choice of Milton's Verse*, introduced and selected, Faber, 1975.
Samuel Johnson, *The History of Rasselas, Prince of Abissinia*, with introduction, Penguin, 1976.
Oxford Book of Contemporary Verse, 1945–1980 (with introduction), OUP, 1980.
Oxford Book of Death (with introduction), OUP, 1983.
Fair of Speech, The Uses of Euphemism, ed. and contributor, OUP, 1985.
Faber Book of Fevers and Frets, Faber, 1989.

NOTES ON CONTRIBUTORS

JOHN BAYLEY is Warton Professor of English and a Fellow of St Catherine's College, Oxford. His works include *The Characters of Love* (1959); studies of Tolstoy and of Pushkin; *Shakespeare and Tragedy* (1980). He is now working on a study of A. E. Housman. His only novel, *In Another Country* (1955), was republished by OUP in their Twentieth-Century Classics series in 1986.

PATRICIA BEER's *Collected Poems*, published by Carcanet in 1988, is soon to appear in a paperback edition. She was one of the poets chosen for inclusion in D. J. Enright's *Oxford Book of Contemporary Verse*, and she also contributed an essay, 'Elizabeth Bennet's Fine Eyes', to *Fair of Speech: The Uses of Euphemism*. She has just finished writing a novel.

A. S. BYATT taught in Art School, and was Senior Lecturer in English at University College London until 1983. She has published five novels, and a book of short stories. Her latest novel, *Possession: A Romance* appears in spring 1990. D. J. Enright was formerly her editor at Chatto & Windus. They went to China on a cultural exchange of writers in 1984.

SHIRLEY CHEW studied at Singapore University and Oxford, and now lectures in English at the University of Leeds. She has published on English and Commonwealth authors, and is the editor of *Arthur Hugh Clough: Selected Poems* and *Re-visions of Canadian Literature*. At the moment she is collaborating on a critical study of new writings in English.

DONALD DAVIE, critic and poet, has most recently published *To Scorch or Freeze: Poems on the Sacred* (1988), and in 1989, *Under Briggflatts: A History of Poetry in Britain 1960–1989*. His *Collected Late Poems* were published by Carcanet who plan a complete poems in late 1990.

DOUGLAS DUNN's most recent books of poems are *Selected Poems* (1986) and *Northlight* (1988). He was the poetry critic for *Encounter* when D. J. Enright was co-editor of the magazine. He lives in Tayport, Fife.

DAVID ELLIS, who teaches at the University of Kent, has taken a special interest in life histories. He has translated Stendhal's *Memoirs of an Egotist*, written a book on Wordsworth's *Prelude*, and has been commissioned by Cambridge University Press to write the third volume (1922–30) of their new biography of D. H. Lawrence.

LEONARD FORSTER is a Fellow of Selwyn College and Emeritus Professor of German in the University of Cambridge. His main interests have been contemporary lyric poetry and seventeenth-century German literature. He has long been one of the editors of *German Life & Letters*. He edited the *Penguin Book of German Verse* in 1957.

P. N. FURBANK is Visiting Professor in Literature at the Open University. His books include *E. M. Forster: A Life* (1977–8), and *Unholy Pleasure: the Idea of Social Class* (1985). He is at present at work on a book on Diderot.

RUSSELL GREENWOOD joined the Diplomatic Service in 1949, and served twice at the Foreign Office Bangkok, in Tokyo, and in Osaka, and also in Rangoon, and antidotally, Rome. He first met D. J. Enright in Japan. Since 1983 he has been Professor of Asian Studies at Matsusaka University, Japan.

KOH TAI ANN is a former pupil of D. J. Enright's in Singapore, where she now teaches in the Department of English Language and Literature.

JEREMY LEWIS was a director of Chatto & Windus from 1979 to 1989. His autobiography, *Playing for Time*, was published in 1987, and he contributed an essay, 'In the Office', to *Fair of Speech: The Uses of Euphemism*. He is a freelance writer and editor, and is at work on a second volume of autobiography.

NAOMI LEWIS is a writer whose medium happens most often to be the critical essay, but with forays into poems and stories. She is known (*inter alia*) as an expert on children's literature. Among recent books are *Messages* (Faber) and *A Footprint on the Air* (both poetry anthologies), and for the young, *Come with Us, Proud Night Fair Lady, Cry Wolf*, and *Johnny Longnose*.

DERWENT MAY was literary editor of *The Listener* from 1965 to 1986. He has published four novels with Chatto & Windus, and studies of Proust and Hannah Arendt. He is now Associate Arts Editor of the *Daily* and *Sunday Telegraph*.

BLAKE MORRISON is the author of *The Movement: English Poetry and Fiction of the 1950s*, first published by OUP in 1980. He has published two collections of poems, and with Andrew Motion co-edited *The Penguin Book of Contemporary Poetry*. He has recently become literary editor of the *Independent on Sunday*.

PETER PORTER has published many books of poetry, since 1970 with OUP. His *Collected Poems* was published in 1983, and his most recent new book is *Possible Worlds* (1989). He met D. J. Enright in 1970 when they toured Israel in a party of British poets. He wrote and presented a special programme about Enright's poetry for the Australian Broadcasting Commission in 1976.

DAVID RAWLINSON taught in the English Department at the University of Singapore from 1960 to 1970, and since then has taught at La Trobe University in Australia. He is the author of *The Practice of Criticism* (1968), and has written on, among others, Pope, Samuel Johnson, Kipling, and Ben Jonson.

JACQUELINE SIMMS is the author of a novel, *Unsolicited Gift* (Chatto, 1982), and has had poems and essays published in magazines. For the academic year of 1984–5 she taught literature at Nara Women's University in Japan. She has been the commissioning editor of OUP's new poetry in two stints: first from 1976 to 1983, and again since 1986. She became D. J. Enright's editor with his *A Faust Book*.

PAUL THEROUX, travel writer and novelist, taught in Singapore during what turned out to be D. J. Enright's last year there. His books include *Saint Jack*, a novel based in Singapore, *The Great Railway Bazaar: By Train Through Asia* (1975); *The Consul's File* (1977), and others. His most recent novel is *My Secret History* (1989).

ANTHONY THWAITE first met D. J. Enright in 1955, when they coincided as lecturers in Japan. Since then he has been in turn a BBC Radio producer, literary editor of *The Listener*, assistant professor of English at the University of Libya, literary editor of *The New Statesman*, and co-editor of *Encounter* when Enright left. He has published many books of poems, most recently *Poems 1953–1988* (Hutchinson 1989).

WILLIAM WALSH is the author of a book, *D. J. Enright: Poet of Humanism* (1974); and other publications include *Coleridge* (1973), F. R. Leavis (1980), *R. K. Narayan* (1982), and *Indian Literature in English* (forthcoming). He is Emeritus Professor of Commonwealth Literature at Leeds University, where he was formerly Chairman of the School of English and Acting Vice-Chancellor.

GAVIN YOUNG met D. J. Enright in Singapore in 1965, while covering various wars in South-East Asia for the *Observer*. Later he wrote *Return to the Marshes* about his life with the Marsh Arabs; *Slow Boats to China* and *Slow Boats Home*; and then *Worlds Apart* (Hutchinson, 1987). He is now back in South-East Asia looking around Joseph Conrad's world for another book.